Luis Jorge Garay Salamanca
Eduardo Salcedo–Albarán
Guillermo Macías Fernández

MACRO-CORRUPTION AND INSTITUTIONAL CO-OPTATION

THE "LAVA JATO" CRIMINAL NETWORK

Collaborators:

Diana Santos Cubides
Nathalia Guerra Villamizar
Laura Rojas Pinilla

Table of Contents

Content

Content

Disclaimer

The facts and analysis presented herein are sustained in files and documents of the Brazilian Public Ministry related to the "Lava Jato" illicit/criminal network and sub-networks analyzed, and sometimes not on definitive judicial decisions. This means that when final sentences are promulgated, modifying the information previously accepted by the first judicial instances, the result and the analysis presented in this book will also change.

In the case of the names mentioned, quoted or referenced, who are accused –with the exception of those specifically mentioned, quoted or referenced in the text as definitively condemned–, the presumption of innocence, in observance of individual rights is always preserved. The judicial truth is the jurisdiction of the courts, which by law will decide whether the defendants are innocent or guilty[1].

It is clarified that *belonging to, participating in, being connected to, or appearing on* the network analyzed herein does not imply having committed any criminal act or being engaged in any criminal enterprise, although the network, as a whole, has an illicit character. It is always possible to *belong, participate, be connected, or appear in* the network as an agent promoting interests that are socially and institutionally beneficial, or as a result of coercion, among other reasons unrelated to criminal acts committed by the agent.

---

1 Based on: Francesco Forgione (2010). Mafia export. Cómo la Ndrangheta, la Cosa Nostra y la Camorra han colonizado el mundo. Anagrama. Crónicas. Barcelona, págs. 11-12.

Introduction

"Lava Jato" is an on-going Federal Police investigation executed for dismantling corruption and money laundering schemes that initially involved Petrobras, the Brazilian State-managed oil company. From 2014 to mid-2017, this operation developed 41 phases of investigation involving private and State companies, high-ranking officials, politicians, business related persons, *doleiros*, and drug traffickers, among other types of agents from 12 countries.

Since the initial complaint sustained by Hermes Freitas Magnus, who owned the Brazilian company "Dunel", along with Maria Teodora Silva, the investigations began, which allowed identifying four criminal groups led by the currency exchange operators Carlos Habib Chater, Alberto Youssef, Nelma Mitsue Penasso Kodama and Raul Henrique Srour. These four criminal structures operated between 2005 and 2014 to obtain millionaire contracts with Petrobras and other State companies through bribe payments to company officials and to politicians with power to appoint those officials. The bribes were so massive, that a complex scheme of money laundering and even trafficking was established to handle the movements of money through several layers of real and façade companies, and through the financial system of various countries.

Considering the amount and diversity of people, companies, financial systems, institutions and countries involved, almost anyone would acknowledge today that the "Lava Jato" operation revealed a massive network of corruption and institutional co-optation. One of the purposes of this book is to analyze and understand, for the first time, the detailed dimensions and scope of that massiveness. As it will be discussed, the result of this analysis revealed a massive structure of corruption, institutional co-optation and money laundering in which around 900 social agents, including individuals and companies, established almost 2,700 interactions, and number of agents and interactions keeps growing as the Brazilian authorities reveal more information.

This analysis is based on records and documents published by the Brazilian judicial system until June of 2017. In a sense, this analysis is about "translating" the judicial truth that the *Ministério Público Federal* revealed, into a single model that can be visualized and analyzed. However, the investigations and prosecutions conducted in Brazil were obviously fragmented, which means that gathering and analyzing all the 150 sources consulted herein, to elaborate and understand the entire network, required a specific protocols and numerous hours of data collection and analysis. At the end, more than 250 Brazilian and foreign companies, 170 individuals specifically related to businesses, and 100 public officials were identified, and that information today relies on a centralized database with the detailed information of each one of those intervening agents.

Considering the massiveness of the identified network and its key sub-networks, their structural impacts on the economic, social and political systems in Brazil, and their engagement on corruption structures across Latin America and on money laundering worldwide, the concept of "macro-corruption" is introduced herein to describe the scope of this phenomenon.

Although bribery was also used to articulate this macro-network, the traditional concept of corruption is insufficient for understanding the dimension and implications of this structure: "Lava Jato" is not just another scandal of corruption in which large amounts of public resources (billions of dollars) were unlawfully re-oriented and appropriated by few powerful individuals; it is a massive and transnational network of corruption that manipulated Brazilian institutions to satisfy few powerful people and their exclusive interests. Therefore, "Lava Jato" is herein conceived and conceptualized as a network of macro-corruption and institutional co-optation; an intricate and perverse system planned and established by politicians, high-ranking public officers and business people to divert and launder large amounts of public resources.

On the other hand, it is necessary to stress that although in modern criminal law the term "crime" does not have a simple and universally accepted definition, for the purpose of this book crime will be understood as an act that is harmful not only for an individual but also for a society and the State. Criminal acts are forbidden and punishable by law. A criminal offense, therefore, is a category created and defined by the criminal law in each. Similarly, an illicit act is committed by someone who knows that the act is prescribed as disallowed by law, but under different circumstances, the same act could be legal. For example, if a group of individuals imports a legal commodity, that action only becomes illicit when specific prescribed procedures are not fulfilled. This means that some actions oscillate in a thin line between a licit and an illicit character; a licit action becomes illicit if certain specifications are not fulfilled or if the consequences of the action are harmful. Bearing this in mind, the "Lava Jato" network is referred herein as illicit/criminal, because some specific actions that will be discussed, cannot be defined as crimes by default, but acquire an illicit character when analyzed in the context of the entire network.

This book has ten chapters. After this introduction, the first chapter discusses how the concept of basic corruption does not explain the complexity of complex corrupt structures such "Lava Jato"; therefore, the concepts of systemic macro-corruption and institutional co-optation are proposed. The second chapter presents some relevant approaches to understand corruption in Brazil, discussing certain recent cases. The third chapter introduces key methodological concepts and describes the basic characteristics of the "Lava Jato" network and its main sub-networks. The fourth chapter is an in-depth analysis of the structure, discussing its most important social agents and interactions established by those agents.

The four following chapters include a detailed analysis of systematic amendments to public contracts, simulation of private contracts, illicit electoral funding and millionaire bribes paid to articulate four main illicit sub-networks of "Lava Jato". The analysis begins in the fifth chapter with the "Petrobras" sub-network, discussing the main interactions that Petrobras officials, private operators and political parties established to articulate the core of corruption that later reproduced across Latin America. Then, the sixth, seventh and eighth chapters analyze the "Eletrobras – Eletronuclear", the "Sergio Cabral", and the "JB" sub-networks. Each sub-network, although focused on specific activities share the similar *modus operandi*: agreements between public servants and political parties to appoint in officials who favored specific companies in tendering processes, on a permanent basis.

A reader who is not concerned on understanding the operative details of the "Lava Jato" network but on its overall structure as well as on its institutional effects, can go directly form the fifth to the ninth chapters. However, public prosecutors, judges, lawyers and scholars interested on understanding the details of these illicit sub-structures will find informative insights about the specific illicit activities that sustained the network.

The ninth chapter synthetizes the concepts of institutional cooptation and macro-corruption according to the evidence presented in the previous chapters. The tenth analyzes the conceptual, methodological and technological reforms required to confront complex networks such as "Lava Jato".

Although some people could assume that the judicial investigations and prosecutions carried out in Brazil are enough for confronting macro-corruption and institutional co-optation, the truth is that the required structural and societal reforms and transformations have not yet happened. For instance, in the near future powerful groups will continue using political parties in most of Latin America, as a tool to promote exclusive, egoistic and even illicit powerful interests, leading to a deep reconfiguration of social institutions and, in the end, to consolidate an unacceptable ineffectiveness of the Rule of Law.

Additionally, institutional mechanisms for transnational investigation and prosecution of macro-corruption do not exist yet; adoption and application of multilateral conventions is the international procedure used today but their scope and effectiveness is far from the required ones. In the meantime, the few local prosecutors and judges who try to confront the phenomenon constantly face legislative, procedural, methodological and technological limitations.

"Lava Jato" is the most complex transnational network of macro-corruption known and investigated to date, but unfortunately it will not be the last one. As the global society keeps evolving toward dynamics of permanent and massive connectivity and fast change, illicit and criminal networks will increase their global scope and, therefore, their levels of resilience. In order to face the radical transformation of culture, societal transformations must be implemented and legislations and judicial systems worldwide must be adjusted and reinterpreted to answer the complex challenges ahead.

Chapter 1. About Corruption

A Preliminary Note

People have often thought that as a rule, criminal or illicit groups –from sporadic gangs to organized criminal structures– confront the State. However, research carried out during recent years shows that the history of relationships between the State and illicit groups is not always of confrontation but on the contrary, of collaboration for mutual benefit.[2] Indeed, sometimes illicit and criminal groups infiltrate and co-opt specific State institutions to achieve their unlawful and illegitimate interests. Even more, some government officials, businesspersons, and politicians in many cases establish agreements and lasting relationships with illicit groups, taking advantage of their power to obtain selfish and illicit benefits that negatively affect public interests. These alliances can be observed even at the highest decision-making levels, affecting the structure and the operation of public and private institutions. Bearing this in mind, the following pages are an analysis of the sophisticated alliances between hundreds of private and public agents, across the lawful and unlawful sectors of society, established for the purpose of wrongfully

---

2 Garay Salamanca, L. J., Salcedo-Albarán, E., & De León Beltrán, I. (2010). *Illicit Networks Reconfiguring States: Social Network Analysis of Colombian and Mexican Cases*. Bogotá: Método Foundation.

appropriating the public budget of Brazil, in a massive and unprecedented way.

The Concept of Corruption

The concept of corruption is used to refer various negative social situations, from institutional vacuums to criminal offenses. In its most basic meaning, corruption is often interpreted as *"the misuse of public office for private gain"*[3] or the abuse of public functions to obtain private and exclusive benefits.[4] Traditional analysis on corruption has focused on how bribery practices allow interactions between public and private agents; in fact, bribery has been interpreted as the main procedure used to establish agreements between public and private agents who obtain benefits by breaking specific laws and norms.

Unfortunately, this definition is misleading in practical terms, since it does not specify when the use of power for private purposes may be interpreted as an "abuse".[5] This definition also implies a dichotomy between the public/impersonal and private/personal spheres and reinforces the idea of keeping them separate, which is often difficult to enforce in practice, as it has been observed in different political contexts. According to the anthropologist Elizabeth Harrison, this dichotomy derives from a Weberian notion that understands bureaucratic organizations as inherently rational-legal; a dichotomy that has its roots in the general rationalist paradigm adopted since Descartes. Nonetheless,

---

3 Rose-Ackerman, S. (1999). *Corruption and Government: Causes, Consequences and Reforms*. New York: Cambridge University Press.
4 World Bank. (1997). *Helping Countries Combat Corruption: The Role of The World Bank*. Washington: World Bank.
5 Dávid-Barrett, E., & Philip, M. (2015). *Realism About Political Corruption*. **Annual Review of Political Science**, 387-402.

for Weber, this was an ideal type that cannot be found empirically in real practice.[6]

Recent literature addresses the link between corruption and formal and operative elements of democracy, such as electoral rules and processes, or the model and level of decentralization.[7] In this context, during the 1990s, political scientist Dennis Thompson proposed the term "institutional corruption" as a necessary step in the process to overcome the individualistic and casual approach dominating the traditional analysis on corruption. Thompson focuses on the impact of corruption on various political processes and institutions. According to the author, an individual advantage is acceptable as long as it contributes to promote competition in the democratic process; otherwise, if it undermines and damages the political process, it cannot be tolerated. In conclusion, the impact of an action is much more important than its intention.[8]

Lawrence Lessig brings a more recent approach to the conceptualization of corruption. According to this author, "institutional corruption" should not be understood as a moral issue about what is good or bad, but as a systemic and strategic influence on institutions that is usually legal and perceived as ethical, even though it compromises the effectiveness of those institutions by diverting them from their fundamental purposes, therefore affecting the public confidence on the institutions' reliability. Likewise, Lessig proposes the need to distinguish between the ordinary meaning of corruption -which he associates with bribery-,

---

6 Harrison, E. (2007). *Corruption. Development in Practice*, 672–678.
7 Bagashka, T. (2014) Unpacking Corruption: The Effect of Veto Players on State Capture and Bureaucratic Corruption. *Political Research Quarterly*, 67(1), 165–180.
8 Dávid-Barrett, E., & Philip, M. (2015). *Realism About Political Corruption. Annual Review of Political Science*, 387–402.

from the activities that effectively undermine the legitimacy and effectiveness of institutions. It should be noted that Lessig's concept of "corrupt action" strongly depends on the purposes of a given institution.[9]

According to Lessig's proposal, the intentions of the subject who commits the act of corruption are also important. Considering that he interprets the systemic and strategic character of the act as a fundamental component of institutional corruption, the individual or group who commits such an act must be aware of and must intend to distort and undermine the institution's purposes.[10]

Concentrating their attention on the actor's intentions, Danila Serra and Leonard Wantchekon propose another definition for corruption: breaking the rules "behind closed doors" for illicit and private advantage.[11] However, secrecy is not a condition fulfilled in all cases of corruption, since often corruption involves public knowledge. This may happen whenever breaking a specific norm is culturally accepted.

To identify the practices of corruption it is important to distinguish between grand corruption and petty corruption. Petty corruption is associated with "street operations" and, therefore, involves more modest amounts of money, as these transactions are typical of low and middle-ranking government officials. On the other hand, according to Martínez García, grand corruption refers to practices perpetrated and reproduced by heads of state, ministers

---

9 Lessig, L. (2013). "Institutional Corruption" defined. *Law Med*, 2-4.
10 Dávid-Barrett, E., & Philip, M. (2015). *Realism About Political Corruption*. **Annual Review of Political Science**, 387-402.
11 Serra, D., & Wantchekon, L. (2012). *New Advances in Experimental Research on Corruption*. Bingley: Emerald Group

and officials in positions of political and administrative power; practices that usually involve large sums of money.[12] Each of these modalities occurs in central, regional or local government levels.[13]

Furthermore, Gervais Rufyikiri explains that grand corruption is executed through (i) intentional irregularities in public contracting, (ii) tax evasion through the manipulation of the value of taxable assets, (iii) the use of fake receipts, (iv) falsified certificates on the origin and identification of imported goods, and (v) abusive tax exemptions.[14] The people responsible, as previously mentioned, are usually politicians and high-ranking officials that accept or demand bribes to implement and cover up irregular procedures. Additionally, businessmen who offer bribes to obtain irregular preferential treatment.

In practice, corruption through the process of public contracts is one of the most used but less sanctioned, since there are realized inter-personal and group negotiations, informal in most cases, and do not fully comply the established rules and standardized processes. According to Rufyikiri corruption through public contracts begins during the preparation phase of a bidding, when it is often designed to fit a specific company, eliminating the competition before the tender even begins. In this process, a portion of the benefits generated by the contracts is distributed among various government officials and, to hide it, several

---

12 Martínez García, D. (2014). *La Corrupción y su efecto retroalimentativo: Una de las mayores amenazas a la democracia. Letras Jurídicas* (29), 107–118.
13 Villoria, M., Van Ryzin, G., & Lavena, C. (2013). Social consequences of government corruption: A study of institutional disaffection in Spain. *Public Administration Review* (73).
14 Rufyikiri, G. (2016). *Grand Corruption in Burundi: a collective action problem which posses major challenges for governance reforms.* Institute of Development Policy (IOB).

mechanisms of concealment and money laundering are put into motion.[15]

Based on these type of activities, the phenomenon of grand corruption is not specific to a certain country or government. For instance, Sonny Shiu-Hing Lo elaborated a comparative case between two locations: Hong-Kong and Macao. In both cases, the author argued that the individual greed of some officials led to the creation of a grand corruption scheme so powerful that neutralized anti-corruption commissions and the scrutiny of mass media. The proceedings that resulted from these operations, were often possible due to the tight personal connections between government officials and business elites.[16]

In other places explored by Rufyikiri, such as Burundi, in Central Africa, it was found that corruption is "rampant and systemic", counteracting almost completely the institutional actions against corruption. In this country, as expected, corruption frustrated good practices of governance and ultimately led to the complete instability of the system, turning it into the world's poorest nation.[17] In this same sense, Hazel Gray argues that in the case of Tanzania, the grand corruption structure involved high-ranked politicians and government officials, domestic and multinational firms in a series of illegal activities that included bribes, embezzlement of public funds and the payment of political favors.[18]

---

15 Ibid.

16 Shiu Hing Lo, S. (2017). *Comparative grand corruption and protection pacts among elites: the cases of Ao Man Long in Macao and Hui Si-Yan in Hong Kong.* **Asian Journal of Political Science**, 25(2), 234-251.

17 Rufyikiri, G. (2016). *Grand Corruption in Burundi: a collective action problem which psoses major challenges for governance reforms.* Institute of Development Policy (IOB).

18 Gray, H. S. (2015). *The political economy of grand corruption in Tanzania.* **African Affairs**, 114(456), 282-403.

Recent Theoretical Approaches to Corruption

State Capture

A recent theoretical approach to corruption and criminality has been developed to understand key contemporary characteristics of the phenomena. It has been proposed a concept defining a specific form of high-scale corruption traditionally referred as State Capture (StC) in countries characterized by severe institutional failures or weakness. Traditional State Capture (StC), which can be understood as an ulterior form of casual and basic corruption, is defined as the intervention of individuals, groups or lawful firms and organizations in the drafting of laws, decrees, regulations, and public policies, in order to obtain long-lasting economic benefits.[19]

The following basic features of traditional StC are often identified: (i) It is the action of lawful groups, (ii) rationalized by economic motivation and looking for economic benefits or advantages, (iii) it happens mainly through bribery at domestic and transnational levels and (iv) it is executed especially over the legislative and administrative branches

---

19 Hellman, J. S., Jones, G., & Kaufmann, D. (2000). "Seize the State, Seize the Day" State Capture, Corruption, and Influence in Transition. The World Bank.
Hellman, J., & Kaufmann, D. (2001). *Confronting the Challenge of State Capture in Transition Economies*. *Finance & Development*, 38(4).
Kaufmann, D., Kraay, A., & Mastruzzi, M. (2010). "The Worldwide Governance Indicators: Methodology and Analytical Issues". World Bank Policy Research Working Paper No. 5430.

at the national level.[20] However, a much more complex type of high-scale corruption can be observed, as discussed in the following chapters.

After analyzing StC situations in States where the Rule of Law is in process of consolidation, it has been found a more advanced and complex type of State or institutional capture in which (i) lawful and also unlawful groups intervene – and not only lawful social agents such as firms–; (ii) not only economic benefits but also judicial and political, and even of social legitimacy are sought; (iii) coercion and political agreements complement and even substitute bribery, and (iv) the sphere of influence happens in different branches and levels of the public administration.[21]

In traditional StC processes, no matter its complexity, a key characteristic is that interactions among social agents are usually established in one direction: from lawful – illicit or criminal– agents who operate outside the State, towards lawful agents who operate inside the State; this characteristic coincides with the literal sense of "Capture" as a process carried out by external social agents.[22]

---

20 Garay Salamanca, L. J., Salcedo-Albarán, E., & De León Beltrán, I. (2010). *Illicit Networks Reconfiguring States: Social Network Analysis of Colombian and Mexican Cases*. Bogotá: Metodo Foundation; Garay Salamanca, L. J., & Salcedo-Albarán, E. (2012). *Narcotráfico, corrupción y Estados*. Bogotá: Debate; &
Garay Salamanca, L. J., & Salcedo-Albarán, E. (2015). *Drug Trafficking, Corruption and States: How Illicit Neoworks Shaped Institutions in Colombia, Guatemala and México*. iUniverse
21 Garay Salamanca, L. J., Salcedo-Albarán, E., & De León Beltrán, I. (2010). *Illicit Networks Reconfiguring States: Social Network Analysis of Colombian and Mexican Cases*. Bogotá: Metodo Foundation.
22 Garay Salamanca, L. J., Salcedo-Albarán, E., & De León Beltrán, I. (2009). *From State Capture towards the Co-opted State Reconfiguration: An Analytical Synthesis*. MÉTODO.
Garay Salamanca, L. J., Salcedo-Albarán, E., & De León Beltrán, I. (2010). *Illicit Networks Reconfiguring States: Social Network Analysis of Colombian and Mexican Cases*. Bogotá: Metodo Foundation

Co-opted State Reconfiguration

Under the same conceptual framework of reference, it has been proposed a category that represents a more advanced and complex form of State and institutional co-optation, in which agents establish agreements in a bi-directional way throughout mechanisms complementing and even substituting traditional bribery. This advanced and complex stage of institutional capture and co-optation has been referenced by Garay *et al.* as Co-opted State Reconfiguration (CStR), which is characterized by deeper and long-lasting impacts on democratic institutions than the ones observed in traditional StC.[23]

Coopted State Reconfiguration has been defined as: "The action of legal and illegal organizations which through illegitimate practices, modify the political and economic regime, from within the State and private sector, to influence systematically on the formulation, modification, interpretation and application of the rules of the game and public policies, in order to obtain sustainable benefits and validate their interest socially, politically and legally, although those interest do not obey the guiding interest of social welfare".[24]

Among its main characteristics, CStR consists of the establishment of bi-directional agreements between agents operating inside the State –such as public officers– at different ranking levels and branches of public

---

23 Ibid.
24 Garay Salamanca, L. J & Salcedo Albarán, E. (2016). *Macro-criminalidad: Complejidad y Resiliencia de las Redes Criminales*. Bloomington: iUniverse. Page 9.
Garay Salamanca, L. J., Salcedo-Albarán, E., & De León Beltrán, I. (2010). *Illicit Networks Reconfiguring States: Social Network Analysis of Colombian and Mexican Cases*. Bogotá: Método Foundation

administration, and social agents operating outside the State, being lawful or unlawful; the latter complement or even supplants bribery in order to obtain selfish benefits and advantages not only of economic nature but also of political and social legitimacy kind, with long-lasting perverse impacts on those institutions involved. [25]

Co-opted State Reconfiguration relates to the instrumental capture of institutions that are critical for the entire social system −such as political parties, civic organizations, media, among others− to reproduce and legitimate unlawful procedures and egoistic benefits and advantages, sacrificing social long-lasting purposes and interests. [26]

Institutional Co-optation

In spite that the original categories refer to State capture and co-optation, as a result of further empirical analyses and researches it has been verified that these processes not only happen in public institutions but also in private ones. For this reason, the categories of capture and co-optation also apply not only to the State, in the sense of public administration, but also to other public and private institutions broadly denominated herein as Co-opted Institutional Reconfiguration (CItR) −or briefly, "Institutional Co-optation". The case analyzed in this book illustrates this type of public and private Institutional Co-optation.

---

25 Garay Salamanca, L. J., & Salcedo-Albarán, E. (2015). *Drug Trafficking, Corruption and States: How Illicit Netoworks Shaped Institutions in Colombia, Guatemala and México.* iUniverse

26 Garay Salamanca, L. J., & Salcedo-Albarán, E. (2012). *Narcotráfico, corrupción y Estados.* Bogotá: Debate.
Garay Salamanca, L. J., & Salcedo-Albarán, E. (2015). *Drug Trafficking, Corruption and States: How Illicit Netoworks Shaped Institutions in Colombia, Guatemala and México.* iUniverse.

In fact, "State Capture", "Coopted State Reconfiguration" and "Coopted Institutional Reconfiguration" are social scenarios in which public and private lawful agents, such as candidates, public officials and businessmen establish agreements and co-opt not only lawful agents but also unlawful agents –such as drug traffickers–, and vice versa, which results in a coordination of mutual interests.

Most of the agents involved in a scheme of Institutional Co-optation can be defined as *grey*. To understand what a grey agent is, it is useful to acknowledge that each node has an institutional and an organizational role; those roles are defined as "functional/institutional" and "functional/organizational" because they consist of a set of "functions" that each agent executes.

The "functional/institutional role of an agent is defined with reference to any action aiming to the promotion or obstruction of some formal or informal institutions, either lawful or unlawful. Those formal and informal institutions can be socially beneficial or socially perverse; therefore, the functional/institutional role can be morally and socially evaluated according to the social benefits generated".[27] On the other hand, the "functional/organizational" role refers to the social group in which the agent operates.

Therefore, the analysis of the functional/organizational and functional/institutional roles allows differentiating between a strictly lawful agent (*bright*), a strictly unlawful agent (*dark*) or an undefined agent (*grey*), as follows:

---

27 Garay Salamanca, L. J. & Salcedo–Albarán, E. (2012). *Narcotráfico, corrupción y Estados*. Bogotá: Debate. p. 49.

· A lawful agent (*bright*) is the one who belongs to a lawful organization and plays a lawful functional/institutional role.

· An unlawful agent (*dark*) is the one who belongs to an unlawful organization and plays an unlawful functional/institutional role, obstructing and promoting non-compliance with lawful institutions.

· An undefined agent (*grey*) is the one whose exercised functions do not fall under either previous situation. A basic example of an undefined, or *grey* agent, is a traffic officer who obstructs compliance with traffic laws while belonging to a lawful organization. As expected, a more dramatic case of a grey agent is observed when a high-rank official, such as a legislator or a president, favors illicit groups.

Systemic Macro-Corruption and Institutional Co-optation: A New Form of Corruption

Conceptualization

Given the amount and diversity of individuals and companies involved, and the amount and diversity of interactions established, a case of "Systemic Macro-Corruption" such as the one herein analyzed is a macro-criminal system, as it has been previously defined.[28] Additionally, given its systematic and increasingly trans-national dimensions "Systemic Macro-Corruption" could also be assimilated

---

28 Garay Salamanca, L. J & Salcedo Albarán, E. (2016). *Macro-criminalidad: Complejidad y Resiliencia de las Redes Criminales*. Bloomington: iUniverse.

to the so-called "Grand Corruption", a concept that unfortunately has not been duly defined. In any case, this phenomenon consists of the active participation of various powerful –public and private– social agents and institutions, at various scales and territories through innovative procedures, agreements, and mechanisms.

The situation of macro-corruption herein analyzed transcends the usual textbook concept that refers to situations between two corrupt individual agents (persons) through bribery, to obtain selfish and unjustifiable economic benefits. Even traditional definitions of systemic corruption seem to lack the transnational scope observed in the "Lava Jato" case.

Therefore, a macro-corruption process characterizes by the planned and coordinated participation of several agents that can be (i) public or private, (ii) individual or organizations such as private companies or corporations, (iii) lawful, unlawful or grey, for executing (iv) various actions, activities, relationships, or agreements. Additionally, macro-corruption usually requires (v) manipulation of norms and procedures, such as public contracting processes, (vi) money laundering through domestic and trans-national financial operations, which imposes obstacles to track them by local/national authorities, (vii) the establishment of façade enterprises and financial offshore funds, not only to obtain short-term profits but more important, (viii) to co-opt institutions and to reproduce stable relationships with, among others, political parties and their leaders by financing electoral campaigns, therefore co-opting not only high-ranking public officers but key public institutions.

It is different to "capture" or "coopt" a single high-rank official than capturing and co-opting a high-rank institution; the later generates permanent selfish benefits for those involved and results of sophisticated forms of corruption beyond a single bribe.

Given the trans-national complexity of the case analyzed, it is required to propose a new heuristic approach to understand its systemic and multi-level functioning as a comprehensive system of agents, purposes, actions, institutions, and territories, among other intervening components. In this sense, it is important to overcome the classic case-to-case epistemological approach through a systemic approach according to the real complex nature of the macro-corruption and institutional co-optation phenomenon. For this reason, as it is discussed in the final chapter, traditional legal codes and anti-corruption measures, civil and penal, should be drastically superseded.

As the reader will note in the following chapters, the "Lava Jato" network of corruption is a representative example of a kind of institutional co-optation and systemic macro-corruption phenomenon.

Main Consequences of Systemic Macro-Corruption and Institutional Cooptation

As it can be expected, as more advanced and complex is the macro-corruption and institutional co-optation process in terms of (i) the spread of institutions, and licit and illicit activities and markets affected, (ii) the variety and number of powerful agents involved including companies and individuals such as businesspersons, politicians and high-ranking officials, (iii) the diversity of types of social relationships –political, entrepreneurial, bureaucratic, institutional, etc.–, (iv) the amplitude of scope, means and purposes, and (v) the degree of operative trans-nationalization, among other factors, *ceteris paribus*, more systemic, deeper, perverse and perdurable its multiple impacts on the political, economic and societal regime will be. Once the process reaches certain level of development, it will probably alter severely basic institutional foundations, not only of the rule of law but also of the capitalist market regime and the democratic system itself.

In its extreme, "Macro-corruption" and "Institutional Co-optation" contribute to advance towards a kleptocratic corporative system governed by selfish and egoistic interests, against the long-lasting societal interests, of powerful colluded capitalists and politicians, or political parties. Due to the co-optation of key institutions, these colluded agents reproduce instrumental markets that are not ruled by free competition among individual economic agents but by imposition based on the relative political and economic power of agents who are members of the dominant corporative system –public contracting is perhaps the most known type of an instrumental market. These agents will operate through several means, from various types of corruption to coercion and intimidation.

Since the colluded powerful agents of the dominant corporative system need to guarantee an effective and sustainable representation and reproduction of their mutual political and economic interests at determinant key public institutions –such as the Presidency or the Congress, among others–, they require to capture and co-opt the electoral process by empowering allied politicians and political parties in the electoral contest trough mechanisms such as financing political campaigns and political parties. In extreme cases, these agents utilize intimidation and violence.

Complementary, in order to auto-protect the system by increasing its resilience, it has to advance in the process of co-optation of key State institutions such as the judiciary; otherwise, the corporative system would remain vulnerable –even more vulnerable, *ceteris paribus*, as greater the effectiveness of the judicial apparatus– depending on the enforcement of the law, in spite of the severe conceptual and practical limitations of traditional penal and civil codes that are still prevalent in most countries. Some insights are detailed in the final Chapter.

One of the main characteristics of this kind of systems is its relative resilience –greater as deeper the institutional co-optation and as more powerful the corporate and political collusion–, which reflects on the obstacles to reverse the process to an original or alternative situation of institutional legitimate consolidation. Consequently, it is necessary to adopt structural social transformations and to apply decisive reforms in several areas of the political, economic, social and cultural spheres, in order to avoid reaching advanced stages of macro-corruption and Institutional Co-optation. In Chapter 10 a few of many required reforms are discussed.

As can be deduced from chapters 5 to 8, the "Lava Jato" structure is a case of a relatively advanced kleptocratic corporative system, but not up to such stage in which some instances of key institutions as the judicial have been successfully co-opted to favor lasting interests of this illicit network of macro-corruption and institutional co-optation in Brazil.

On the other hand, there should be stressed some of the most important consequences of a relative advanced institutional co-optation of the State by powerful selfish private interests –especially if it is under a kleptocratic corporative system: for instance, the fact that it tends to " (...) decompose the society and the markets, (...) political parties, social classes and ideological adscriptions,"[29] promoting double ideological, social and political adscriptions, and consequently fragmenting and weakening the political system.

In fact, the advancement of this process in favor of powerful private groups has long-lasting fundamental impacts on the functioning of a democratic system and a market regime, by reproducing values and behaviors against: (i) the civic culture and the moral capacities of the citizens, (ii) the preeminence of the public sphere and the public interests over egoistic and excluding private interests, and (iii) the consolidation of an equitable and competitive market and a democratic order in their economic, political and social instances.

Then, the Rule of Law and the citizens' fidelity to the State are affected strengthening the instrumental individualism and weakening the State through its capture or institutional co-optation, at stages beyond the

---

29 Sapelli, G. (1998). *Cleptocracia. El "mecanismo" de la corrupción entre política y economía.* Ed. Losada S. A. Buenos Aires.

basic phenomenon of "clientelism".[30] Simultaneously, it reproduces a tendency to concentrate economic and political power and opportunities, and to aggravate the level of poverty and income inequality, in the opposite direction required for the construction and deepening of a real democracy and a pure competitive market system. Furthermore, it contributes to the empowerment and reproduction of illegality phenomena such as macro-corruption, degrading the prevalence and due observance of the rule of law and the legitimation of the State.

Consequently, given that some markets are therefore regulated not by free competition between economic agents but by coercion and imposition to favor some powerful private interests, therefore breaking the principles of equity, confidence and reciprocity, there is a tendency to create "inequitable instrumental markets" rather than "equitable free-competitive markets", favoring the preeminence of irregular, illicit and criminal practices in the functioning of markets, and as a consequence breaking the basis of the expected free-market regime[31], as a sample of some comprehensive societal and structural transformations reproduced by the kind of social phenomenon like the macro-corruption and institutional co-optation under reference.

---

30 Garay Salamanca, L. J. (1999). *Construcción de una nueva sociedad*. Tercer Mundo Editores-Cambio. Bogotá, and Garay Salamanca, L. J. (2014). "Sobre la problemática de la propiedad y el uso de la tierra en un contexto de usufructo del poder y la violencia como en Colombia. A propósito de algunas perspectivas clásicas de economía política". Bogotá, agosto (recently published, March 2018, as Working Paper by Vortex Foundation).
31 Garay Salamanca, L. J. (1999). *Construcción de una nueva sociedad*. Tercer Mundo Editores-Cambio. Bogotá, and Garay Salamanca, L. J. (2014). "Sobre la problemática de la propiedad y el uso de la tierra en un contexto de usufructo del poder y la violencia como en Colombia. A propósito de algunas perspectivas clásicas de economía política". Bogotá, agosto (recently published, March 2018, as Working Paper by Vortex Foundation).

Chapter 2. Corruption in Brazil

Two of the most accepted indicators of corruption worldwide are the Governance Indicators generated by the World Bank and the Perception Index of Corruption (PIC) generated by International Transparency; the latter has been interpreted as a relatively reliable indicator because comparative studies have shown that "people share a similar notion of corruption across different cultures",[32] although it is considered that its explanatory capacity diminishes severely in hybrid regimes and so-called "young democracies" where corrupt behavior was a common characteristic of authoritarian regimes.[33]

Regarding the Governance Indicators,[34] the "control of corruption" indicator reflects how Brazilians and international experts and survey respondents interpret the quality of anti-corruption measures. In the case of Brazil, this specific indicator has decreased since 2011, when the peak of the decade 2006-2016 was registered, with 63 points. In fact, 2016 is the year with the lowest indicator of 38, which is considerably lower than the 54 points registered as a mean for the Latin America region.

---

32 Tverdova, Y. V. (2011). See No Evil: Heterogeneity in Public Perceptions of Corruption. *Canadian Journal of Political Science / Revue canadienne de science politique, 44(1), 1-25. p. 17.*
33 Sharafutdinova, G. (2010). What Explains Corruption Perceptions? The Dark Side of Political Competition in Russia's Regions. *Comparative Politics, 42(2), 147-166.*
34 Kaufmann, D., Kraay, A., & Mastruzzi, M. (2010). *The Worldwide Governance Indicators: Methodology and Analytical Issues.* World Bank Policy Research Working Paper No. 5430.

The decreasing tendency of the indicator, therefore, coincides with the scandals revealed as result of the "Lava Jato" operations; since the indicator does not inform about the level of corruption but about the quality of controls, this coincidence could reflect frustration with the low quality of controls before the scandals erupted. In this sense, probably it will take years before the indicator increases as result of appreciation towards the judicial measures that Brazilian authorities have enforced to confront corruption.

On the other hand, the Perception Index of Corruption has oscillated around 38 points in 2011, and 40 points in 2016, which means that it has not been drastically affected by the macro-corruption scandals recently revealed. In fact, with 40 points and the 79th place among 176 countries, in 2016 Brazil continued registering a better indicator than Paraguay with 30 points and the 123rd place, Bolivia with 33 points and the 113th place, Peru with 35 points and the 101st place, and Colombia with 37 points and the 90th place. In spite of all, among its neighboring countries, Brazil only lies behind Uruguay with 71 points and the 21st place.[35]

Public Sector

The specialized literature on grand corruption is scarce in Brazil, due to the absence of comparative and distinctive analysis between grand or petty corruption. Nonetheless, as a general concept, corruption has been explored from various perspectives. On one hand, based on economics and political science analyses, Claudio Ferraz and Frederico Finan have found that in Brazil citizens vote as a rational

---

35 Transparency International (2017) Corruption Perception Index for 2016 by Transparency International. Retrieved from: https://transparencia.org.es/wp-content/uploads/2017/01/tabla_sintetica_ipc-2016.pdf

decision to favor those candidates not associated with corruption.[36]

Regarding quantitative investigations, Antonio Carlos de Azevedo and Maria Fernanda Colaco studied the existing links between parliamentary amendments relative to deletion, modification or addition to public project or federal budgets and episodes of municipal corruption in Brazil. They observed that several public officials introduced amendments to public investment projects in order to illicitly enriching themselves.[37]

Through statistics by the National Comptroller's Program against Corruption, such as public draws for surveillance, the authors evaluated the hypothesis that municipalities that receive budget through amendments showed worse corrupt performance. After following up on the socioeconomic and political variables of the cities that received funds for amendments, it was found that their corruption rates were 25% higher than in the case of other cities included in the sample. According to this data, the authors argued that corruption increases when municipalities receive extraordinary monetary transfers. From the authors' perspective, corruption is directly related to institutional fragility, allowing that the execution of the federal budget could be affected by few public officers who seek egoistic and unjustifiable benefits for themselves.

On the other hand, Sergio Praça analyzed the hypothetical relationship between corruption and institutional design,

---

36 Ferraz, C., & Finan, F. (2011). *Electoral Accountability and Corruption: Evidence from the Audits of Local Governments. American Economic Review, 101(4).*
37 Azevedo Sodré, A., & Colaço, M. F. (2010). *Relação entre Emendas Parlamentares e Corrupção Municipal no Brasil: Estudo dos Relatórios do Programa de Fiscalização da Controladoria-Geral da União. RAC – Revista De Administração Contemporânea, 414–433.*

focusing on both: the direct impact of corruption in budgetary processes, and the indirect effects of publicizing the corruption scandals on institutional design. At the first stage, Praça defines corruption as a dependent variable, centralized or decentralized, and at the second stage, corruption is approached as an independent variable. The author concluded that decentralized institutions tend to observe fewer cases of corruption, and that exposure of corruption scandals may promote institutional changes that would considerably affect budgetary processes.[38]

Considering another perspective, Emilson Lopes investigated scandals of political corruption in Brazil from a sociological perspective. The author argued that corruption would be better understood if it is addressed from the moral rationale of the people who commit such actions, or how those actors justify their corruption actions, concluding that people implicated in acts of corruption argue that there is a moral perspective that alleviates individual responsibility, to the point that they consider as a failure their incapacity to know "when to stop".[39]

Furthermore, from a judicial perspective, Mariana Prado, Lindsey Carson and Izabela Correa have argued that in Brazil the fight against corruption has progressed substantially, related to the adoption of innovative supervision and investigation systems, in spite that these controls have not persuaded corrupt agents. For the authors, this is partly explained by failures in the prevalent institutional arrangement, such as poor articulation among

---

38 Praça, S. (2011). *Corrupção e reforma institucional no Brasil, 1988-2008. Opiniao Publica.* Vol. 17 Issue 1, 137-162
39 Lopes, E. (2010). "As gramáticas morais da corrupção: aportes para uma sociologia do escândalo". *Teoria Política e Social na Contemporaneidade,* 126-147.

investigative institutions and the judicature, a judicial body in charge of setting penalties. They have also claimed that the judicature is a weak institution and, therefore, to avoid the limitations of the Brazilian courts, penalties are more dependent on administrative than penal sanctions against corruption.[40]

In order to combat corruption, among other objectives, according to Fernando Filgueiras and Ana Luiza Melo, Brazil has experienced institutional reforms since 1990, when several innovations in public administration have been applied.[41] The administrative reorganization in Brazil has centered on high-ranking public officials with minimal impact on the medium- and low- ranking administrative levels. Bribing practices among public servants and citizens are still common, to the point that reforms in public administration have not produced relevant transformations on the citizens' perception of corruption in Brazil.

Private Organizations and Political Systems

Regarding corruption in private organizations, Renato Almeida, Arnoldo de Hoyos, Cristina Sanches and Ben Hur Ferraz evaluated the susceptibility of leaders to break organizational rules that compromise ethical values. This quantitative research, based on social statistical analysis and descriptive data provided by a company specialized in risk-reduction, *Tic Global*, analyzed a sample of 74 private

40 Mota Prado, M., Carson, L., & Correa, I. (2015). *The Brazilian Clean Company Act: Using Institutional Multiplicity for Effective Punishment. Osgoode Legal Studies Research Paper*, 48.
41 Filgueiras, F., & Aranha, A. (2011). Controle da corrupção e burocracia da linha de frente: regras, discricionariedade e reformas no Brasil. *Dados*, 54.

enterprises based in Brazil and 7276 individuals linked to them. According to the indicators examined, it is suggested that organization leaders tend to relax their ethical principles due to day-to-day professional routines.[42]

Grasping probable causes of corruption in Brazil, Mariana Batista hypothesized that corruption has permeated entire sectors of the State through the operation of networks involving public and private agents. To study this phenomenon, Batista analyzed the dynamics of political competition in the country. The author defined corruption as "the transaction between a politician and a private actor, in which the former transfers a physical property or an unlawful right of ownership of a determinant private actor, in exchange for material or electoral gains."[43]

To determine the influence of (i) re-election, (ii) margin of victory, (iii) opposition power and (iv) partisan coalition on political corruption, Batista analyzed data generated by the Brazilian Institute of Geography and Statistics [*Instituto Brasileiro de Geografia e Estatística*] and the Superior Electoral Court [*Tribunal Superior Electoral*].

Regarding the first variable, the re-election,[44] Batista showed that reelected mayors are characterized by higher levels of corruption during their second administration, and also that politicians who run for re-election are more likely to be corrupt. Despite being restricted to Brazilian data, this finding is also relevant to understand why prominent levels

---

42 Almeida dos Santos, R., de Hoyos Guevara, A. J., Sanches Amorim, M. J., & Ferraz-Neto, B. (2012). Compliance and leadership: the susceptibility of leaders to the risk of corruption in organizations. *Einstein* (São Paulo) vol.10 no.1.

43 Batista, M. (2013). Incentivos da dinâmica política sobre a corrupção, Reeleição, competitividade e coalizões nos municípios brasileiros. *Revista Brasileira de Ciências Sociais*, 87-106.

44 Using data from the IBGE, Profile of the Municipalities of Brazil.

of corruption are observed in countries where mayors can be reelected without limit of terms, such as in Guatemala. Batista analyzed the second variable, the margin of victory, in relation to electoral competitiveness under the majority rule at the level of Brazilian municipalities. Since elections for mayor increase uncertainty of the election results, electoral competitiveness is a restriction on corrupt behavior because corruption may result in loss of votes for the candidate. However, based on data of the Higher Electoral Tribunal, she shows a tendency to higher levels of corruption in order to guarantee a greater margin of electoral victory.[45]

The third variable, the opposition force, was defined as the monitoring and accountability function exerted by opposition parties on the public administration. Batista's hypotheses are that a large number of opposition parliamentarians that confront a mayor may increase the costs of public corruption and that a less fragmented opposition may promote a more restrictive behavior of the rulers, bearing in mind that fewer parties reduce the costs of collective action; therefore, a greater number of parties in the opposition force tends to favor greater levels of corruption.

The fourth variable, political coalition, is particularly important to understand the structure of influence peddling and payment or exchange of political favors that happen in the Brazilian political system. In the municipal political systems, voters tend to elect the mayor and coalition members tend to elect the legislative through the proportional method. Therefore, the concentration of

---

45 Batista, M. (2013). *Incentivos da dinâmica política sobre a corrupção, Reeleição, competitividade e coalizões nos municípios brasileiros.* Revista Brasileira de Ciências Sociais, 87-106.

political responsibility can be empowered by a governmental multi-party coalition that affects the control of the acting government by opposition parties and coalitions. Likewise, the relation of exchange of favors and privileges between the executive power and his multi-party coalition is also relevant, considering that a set of parties with different programmatic positions and preferences are part of the government and, consequently, would control economic and political rents.[46]

According to Batista, "a coalition government must be understood as a government with several parties in power"[47], which means several parties with control of rents and privileges, facilitating the reproduction of corrupt practices.

Electing Corrupt Officials

Regarding why people elect corrupt officials, it has been found that an increased level of perceived corruption affects the electoral turnout: as corruption increases, the percentage of voters decreases.[48] However, in several countries –Brazil included– scandals of corruption are not only constantly revealed but increasingly complex; in fact, it seems that situations of corruption have aggravated in Brazil after the transition to democracy. To answer why voters keep electing corrupt officials, Winters and Weitz-Shapiro propose two hypothetic explanations: first, an information hypothesis by which it is argued that voters elect corrupt politicians when lacking enough information

---

46 Ibid.

47 Ibid, page 100.

48 Stockemer, D., LaMontagne, B., & Scruggs, L. (2013). *Bribes and ballots: The impact of corruption on voter turnout in democracies.* International Political Science Review / Revue internationale de science politique, 34 (1), 74 - 90.

to recognize the involvement of the candidate in acts of corruption; second, a tradeoff hypothesis by which it is stated that corrupt candidates are elected because voters expect "that the overall benefits from a politicians term in office will be greater than the cost associated with corruption."[49]

At least in principle, the popular idea that "*rouba, mas faz*" would support the trade-off hypothesis in Brazil. In fact, surveys from 2000, 2002 and 2007 documented that "a politician who carries out a lot of public works, even if he robs a little, is better than a politician who carries out a few public works and does not rob at all". In contrast, after collecting data in Brazil, the authors found evidence that Brazilians are highly sensitive to information about corruption and react negatively to corrupt officials even if they deliver public goods and services, therefore supporting the information hypothesis, although the negative reactions could diminish among the lowest-income groups of the population.[50]

Corruption in Brazil Before Lava Jato

In October 2002 Luiz Inácio Lula da Silva was elected as the president of Brazil as a leader of the *Partido dos Trabalhadores* [the Workers' Party, PT]. As a working-class man, Lula represented the ideas of a renewed left supposedly more democratic and inclusive, and promoted a 'new unionism'. His eventual election caused strong negative reactions among the right-wing, fearing prejudicial effects on markets. Against all odds, Brazil experienced an impressive

---

49 Weitz-Shapiro, R., & Winters, M. S. (2013). *Lacking information or condoning corruption: When will voters support corrupt politicians? Comparative Politics* 45 (4), 418-436. p. 418.
50 Ibid. p. 418

economic expansion between 2003 and 2013.[51] However, Brazilian economic growth and institutional legitimacy were threatened by the strongly entrenched practices of corruption that probably increased during the last governments.

The political agendas of Lula da Silva and Dilma Rousseff created optimism on resolving Brazilian problems, including chronic corruption; however, the scandals that now involve both of them seem to show that corruption has damaged nuclear democratic institutions such as the Presidency and the Congress of Brazil, deteriorating furthermore its imperfect democracy and the level of legitimacy of political institutions.

While Brazil has confronted corruption during most of its political history, the issue acquired a particularly prominent position in the country's politics since its return to democracy in 1988. Numerous scandals at the federal, state, and municipal levels and across different branches of the public administration confirm that corruption remains as a prominent phenomenon of the country's political system.[52] An emblematic case took place in 2002 when Fernando Collor, the first democratically elected president after over twenty years of military dictatorship, was removed from power after proving his participation in a corrupt influence-peddling scheme to benefit private interests.[53]

---

51 World Bank. (2017). *World Development Indicators GDP Brazil.* Source: https://goo.gl/jcSgqt

52 Carson, L., & Mota Prado, M. (2014). *Mapping corruption and its institutional determinants in Brazil. International Research Initiative on Brazil and Africa. IRIBA Working Paper: 08.*

53 Hipólito, M. (2016) Democracy in Brasil: Has anything changed since the early 1990s?. Latin American Research Centre. University of Calgary. Available in: https://larc.ucalgary.ca/publications/democracy-brazil-has-anything-changed-early-1990s

More recently, in May 2005 came to light the first revelations of a corruption scandal involving Lula and other figures of the PT, leading to a crisis described as "the most extensive in the whole history of the Brazilian Republic".[54] The scandal was known as *"Escândalo do Mensalão"*, consisting on a series of unjustified payments to fund certain political campaigns and to assure loyalty to the government and sustainable alliances between some political parties and the PT.[55]

On the first chapter of the *"Escândalo do Mensalão"*, authorities found monthly payments of approximately USD$ 47,731 to deputies allied to the government, as an exchange for their support. Also, in Minas Gerais, an illegal fund-raising scheme was set up for the 1998 campaign of governor Eduardo Azeredo, who sought reelection in that state. In both cases, 1998 and 2005, the publicist Marcos Valério was identified as coordinator and administrator of the collected resources.[56]

During the investigation, the Federal Police confirmed the operation of a bribe payments scheme involving the Federal District Government (GDF) and service contractors and providers that paid to obtain undue advantages. The companies involved were Infoeducacional, Vertax, Adler, and Linknet. Additionally, more than twelve political parties were allegedly involved in the scheme, especially

54 Flynn, P. (2005). *Brazil and Lula, 2005: crisis, corruption and change in political perspective. Third World Quarterly*, 26(8), 1221-1267(47). Available in: https://doi.org/10.1080/01436590500400025

55 El País. (2006). El Congreso brasileño pide el procesamiento de decenas de políticos. El País. 31 de March de 2006. Available in: https://elpais.com/diario/2006/03/31/internacional/1143756016_850215.html

56 Jusbrasil. (2010). *Doze partidos têm histórico de "mensalões". Jusbrasil.* Source: https://oab-ma.jusbrasil.com.br/noticias/2027976/doze-partidos-tem-historico-de-mensaloes

members of the Brazilian Democratic Movement Party (PMDB) and the Liberal Party in the Chamber of Deputies; in total, 40 individuals were involved in the complaint. Both the defendant and others within the PT declared that the president of the Republic at that moment (Lula da Silva) and the national leadership of the PT did not know about any scheme of payments and benefits to buy political support among members of the Legislative Power.[57] The president of the Liberal Party, on his side, declared the opposite arguing that Lula da Silva was aware of the unlawful association since the beginning of his mandate;[58] however, the involvement of Lula has not been confirmed.

The trial of *Mensalão* began in August 2012 at the Federal Supreme Court (STF), seven years after the initial complaint. At that time, there were 38 individuals in the trial, since one of them died in 2010 and another had its proceedings cancelled. At the end, 27 individuals were convicted on allegations of active and passive corruption, money laundering, embezzlement, tax evasion, foreign exchange infractions and organized crime. José Dirceu, minister of the Civil House, Delúbio Soares, treasurer of the PT, and Jose Genoino, president of the PT, had custodial sentences, as several other businessmen involved on the prosecution.[59]

The trail of the *Mensalão* revealed several scandals of corruption in Brazilian public institutions. There were unlawful payment schemes that included bribes, frauds

---

57 Ibid.

58 El País. (2006). El Congreso brasileño pide el procesamiento de decenas de políticos. *El País*. 31 de March de 2006. Available in: https://elpais.com/diario/2006/03/31/internacional/1143756016_850215.html

59 Jusbrasil. (2010). *Doze partidos têm histórico de "mensalões"*. Jusbrasil. Source: https://oab-ma.jusbrasil.com.br/noticias/2027976/doze-partidos-tem-historico-de-mensaloes

and suspicious transactions; also, clandestine schemes that shared one element in common: important amounts of money circulated between public institutions and agencies and the PT [*Partido dos Trabalhadores*]. After two years of investigations related to PT members, in 2014 the Operation "Car Wash" ["*Lava Jato*"] uncovered a massive corruption structure that led, among other factors, to the current political and economic crisis in Brazil, involving government officials, business leaders, and the state-controlled oil company, Petrobras. More than 100 persons of interest including high-level politicians and top executives of some of the richest corporations in Brazil were imprisoned during the ongoing investigation on the Petrobras scandal. In addition, 16 corporations are still under prosecution.[60]

By the time of the "Car Wash" investigation, Dilma Rousseff was holding the presidency and Brazil faced one of the worst economic recession in years, aggravated by a high fiscal deficit as well as by a rapid increase of public debt and its service (total payment of interests and amortizations). In addition, the real GDP contracted 5.9 percent in the fourth quarter of 2015, worsening from the 4.5 percent decline in the third quarter, the sharpest contraction in a quarter since the early 1990s, when Brazil was still struggling by hyperinflation. Since the first quarter of 2014 up to the fourth quarter of 2015, the real GDP fell 7.2 percent, severely affecting private consumption and investment. In fact, private consumption decreased 6.8 in the fourth quarter of 2015, while gross fixed capital formation contracted 18.5 percent during the same quarter.[61]

60 Hipólito, M. (2016). *Democracy in Brazil: Has anything changed since the early 1990s? Latin American Research Centre.* Source: https://larc.ucalgary.ca/publications/ democracy-brazil-has-anything-changed-early-1990
61 Barua. (2016). *Brazil: Yearning for the good times. Global Economic Outlook,* Q2 2016. Deloitte University Press.

To confront the deteriorated economic situation, former president Rousseff proposed a program of macroeconomic adjustment to control inflation and to drastically reduce fiscal and external imbalances;[62] however, efforts to restrain spending and reduce inflation failed to restore investors' confidence. After the government's failed attempts to energize the economy, the popularity of Rousseff rapidly deteriorated.

Later, during the second year of her second administration, Rousseff was accused of manipulating the federal budget to conceal the aggravation of the country's mounting deficits. Institutional oversight on the presidents' actions strengthened since the former president Collor incident, therefore those irregular presidential actions were not overlooked. On April 17th, 2016, 367 out of the 513 deputies of the Lower House of the Senate in Brazil voted for her suspension, and on May 12th, 2016, the Upper House approved an impeachment motion. Since then, Rousseff has been "temporarily" replaced by Vice-President Michel Temer.[63]

During the "Car Wash" trials, former president Lula da Silva was sentenced to nine years in prison for passive corruption and money laundering. The evidence confirmed bribes for approximately USD$ 1,1 million paid by the company OAS. Specifically, those bribes were invested in a property in Sao Paulo with the titularity of OAS, inhabited

62 Paraguassu, L., & Soto, A. (2016). *Brazil's Temer calls for unity, confidence for Brazil recovery*. *Reuters*. Source: https://www.reuters.com/article/us-brazil-politics/brazils-temer-calls-for-unity-confidence-for-brazil-recovery-idUSKCN0Y206H

63 Hipólito, M. (2016). *Democracy in Brazil: Has anything changed since the early 1990s? Latin American Research Centre*. Source: https://larc.ucalgary.ca/publications/democracy-brazil-has-anything-changed-early-1990s

by Lula da Silva and his family.[64] Like in the *Mensalão* incident, the bribery structure was established to influence governmental decisions, reproduce political alliances and guarantee benefits in favor of personal interests.

This scheme of bribes in exchange of political support may represent a pattern of corruption in Brazil, probably as one of the consequences of the highly fragmented party system which forces presidents to establish several coalitions to guarantee its governance, reproducing the so-called "coalition presidentialism" governing style. For instance, Michel Temer, current president of Brazil, was the vice president of Dilma Rousseff, despite being ascribed to historically antagonistic political parties.[65] The fragile alliance between them finally ended when Dilma Rousseff faced the impeachment process, Temer declared publicly against her and did everything he could to remove her out of the presidency.[66]

Other political characteristic that may have affected the transparency of political institutions in Brazil, contributing to the current political and institutional crisis, is the influence of private corporations on popular elections. For instance, key corporations funded the 2010 presidential campaign of winner Dilma Rouseff, providing nearly 98% of her total provisions, as well as to her main opponent (95.5%). Brazilian corporations can provide up to 2% of

---

64 Gallas, D. (2017). *Brazil's Odebrecht corruption scandal. BBC News.* Source: http://www.bbc.com/news/business-39194395

65 Hipólito, M. (2016). Democracy in Brazil: Has anything changed since the early 1990s? *Latin American Research Centre.* Source: https://larc.ucalgary.ca/publications/democracy-brazil-has-anything-changed-early-1990s

66 Hérmida, X. (2017). *El Supremo de Brasil coloca a Temer al borde de la destitución. El País.* 19th May. Available in: https://elpais.com/internacional/2017/05/18/actualidad/1495118590_847067.html

their gross annual revenues directly to candidates, and therefore their contributions have much more influence than those provided by individuals. In fact, during the 2006 election, 55% of donations to federal deputy candidates originated in corporate donors, while 34% originated in individuals.[67] Corporations consider that electoral donations are financial investment for corporate interests.[68]

In addition to the economic deficit and the corruption scandals shaking Brazilian democratic institutions, the growing lack of confidence in political institutions and the government fueled and aggravated the current crisis. According to the 2014 Edelman Trust Barometer, Brazil exhibited the largest gap between trust on private businesses and trust and confidence on ruling government among the BRIC[69] countries, with only 34 percent of surveyed Brazilians expressing confidence on their government in comparison to 70 percent who trusted on business institutions.[70]

Since 2013 the social discontent has been expressed through massive protests against the government, when the country was getting ready to host the Soccer World Cup, 2014. Specifically, on July 2013 in Rio, more than 300,000 people protested against corruption, police brutality, poor public services, and excess spending on the World Cup.[71]

---

67 Boas, T., Hidalgo, F., & Richardson, N. (2014). *The Spoils of Victory: Campaign Donations and Government Contracts in Brazil. The Journal of Politics* 76(02). Source: https://www.researchgate.net/publication/267796197_The_Spoils_of_Victory_Campaign_Donations_and_Government_Contracts_in_Brazil
68 Mota Prado, M., Carson, L., & Correa, I. (2015). *The Brazilian Clean Company Act: Using Institutional Multiplicity for Effective Punishment. Osgoode Legal Studies Research Paper,* 48
69 Brazil, Russia, India, China.
70 Pew Global. (2014). *Brazilian Discontent Ahead of World Cup.* Available in: http://www.pewglobal.org/2014/06/03/brazilian-discontent-ahead-of-world-cup
71 Watts, J. (2013). *Brazil erupts in protest: more than a million on the streets. The Guardian.* Available in: https://www.theguardian.com/world/2013/jun/21/brazil-police-crowds-rio-protest

Four years later, social mobilization was still popular to protest against the social, economic and political crisis in the country.

In 2017, protests focused on demanding to impeach Michael Temer over corruption allegations, which aggravated the lack of the president's popularity due to the announcements of reducing public investment to confront macroeconomic imbalances. Social mobilizations accentuated and with them a negative, often violent, response from the government. For instance, in May 2017, by order of President Michael Temer, the National Army confronted a riot in Brasilia, a decision that led to 49 citizens injured and produced strong criticism among the opposition and the parties that still support the president.[72]

In brief, corruption scandals that have involved the last presidents of Brazil, among several high-ranking public servants and key corporative agents, among other endemic fractures of the socio-economic system, have broadly affected the legitimacy of institutions, deteriorating confidence on government and affecting the core values of democracy. As discussed in the following chapters, these social, economic and political fractures have aggravated – and will continue to aggravate- as far as corruption keeps reaching the core of public institutions.

---

72 Bedinelli, T., & Benites, A. (2017). *Las protestas contra el presidente Temer paralizan el Gobierno de Brasil. El País.* 25th May. Source: https://elpais.com/internacional/2017/05/24/actualidad/1495652623_766724.html

Chapter 3. The "Lava Jato" Structure

Social Network Analysis

Social Network Analysis (SNA) is a collection of concepts and procedures that facilitate an understanding of social interactions among individuals or groups. In this book, SNA is complemented with protocols developed by Vortex Foundation to illustrate how social agents interacted over a period of time to accomplish illicit or criminal objectives.

The social agents participating in this network were classified under categories that will be explained in the following sections and generated according to the analyzed sources. The interactions established by those social agents were also classified under three main categories or dimensions: (i) *Economic interactions*, which groups sub-categories consisting of the movements of money and financial transactions, (ii) *political interactions*, which groups interactions established *with* and *among* political leaders, candidates, and some public officials, and (iii) *violent and coercive interactions*. Although interactions can be usually classified under any of these categories, there are cases in which additional categories, to be explained below, were applied.

Through algorithms, SNA allows identifying the relevant agents intervening in the network, the sub-networks, the emerging structures, the types of social agents and the types of relationships to be highlighted. In the present analysis, the "relevant" social agents are (i) the 'hub' of the network, in which direct interactions are concentrated, and (ii) the structural bridge with the highest capacity to arbitrate the flows of resources such as money and information. Due to the possibilities of analysis and visualization, SNA has been used to analyze the structure and characteristics of illicit and criminal networks.[73]

The Graph

The illicit structure analyzed in this book required a large number of interactions of collaboration or confrontation, therefore, the situation can be analyzed as a social network: "Social networks can be defined as a group of collaborating (and/or competing) entities that are related to each other."[74] Social networks are analyzed through *nodes* that represent individuals and *lines* or *arcs* that represent the interactions or ties; therefore, "(...) a network is defined as a set of nodes connected by ties."[75]

The "Lava Jato" Network was modeled through a technology of analysis and graphing also developed by

---

73 Morselli, C. (2008) *Inside Criminal Networks.* Montreal: Springer.
Garay Salamanca, L. J. & Salcedo-Albarán, E. (2012). *Narcotráfico, corrupción y Estados.* Bogotá: Debate. Johnson, J. A., R. J., Norwood, B. F., McCoy, D. M., Cummings, B., & Tate, R. R. (2013). *Social Network Analysis: A Systematic Approach for Investigating.* FBI Law Enforcement Sent Bulleting.
74 den Bossche & Segers, (2013). *Transfer of training: Adding insight through social network analysis. Educational Research Review.* 37-47.
75 Worell, J., Wasko, M., & Johnstn, A. (2013). *Social Network Analysis in Accounting Information Systems Research. International Journal of Accounting Information Systems* (14), 127-137.

Vortex Foundation. The technology, consisting of protocols for analyzing, processing and categorizing the already mentioned information, generates a database of nodes and interactions that allows subsequently analyzing characteristics related to specific nodes or interactions.

The first protocol for analyzing sources of information consists of identifying "relationships" or "interactions" between two nodes/agents, according to the following grammar structure:

[[Name Actor 1[Description Node/Agent 1]][interaction[verb/action]]

[[Name Node/Agent2[Description Node/Agent 2]]]

Each syntactic section of this grammar structure is included and processed in the system, through specific protocols that consolidate the database that is then analyzed through additional protocols to generate SNA graphs such as those presented in the following chapters, and to calculate and identify the centrality of each node/agent.

In this analysis, each node represents a social agent; therefore, the concept of "node/agent" is used to identify each individual or corporation participating in the network. Then, each line connecting two nodes/agents represents a social interaction, while the arrow in the line represents the specific direction of that interaction: "For instance, if the node/agent X interacts *with/to* node/agent Z, then there is an arrow from a node representing X to a node/agent representing Z."[76]

---

76 Salcedo-Albarán, E., Goga, K., & Goredema, K. (2014). *Cape Town's underworld mapping a protection racket in the central business district.* Petroria: Institute for Security Studies.

Indicators of Direct Centrality and Betweenness

It is important to differentiate two meanings of centrality: First, the most connected node/agent and second the node/agent with the highest capacity to intervene or arbitrate in the indirect routes of the network.

The direct centrality indicator allows identifying the number of direct interactions established by each node/agent. For instance, in the Figure 0 the node/agent 1 has 4 direct interactions, while the nodes 2, 3, 4 and 5 only have one direct interaction with the node/agent 1. Since there is a total of 8 unidirectional interactions, the node/agent 1 concentrates 50% (4) of the total direct interactions, while each of the nodes/agents 2, 3 and 4 concentrate 12,5%. In this social situation, the node/agent 1 is the hub of Figure 0 because it registers the highest direct centrality indicator.

Figure 0. A graph with 5 interacting nodes/agents

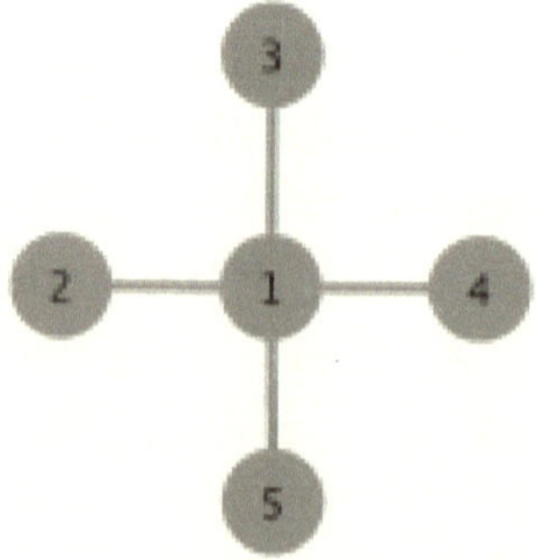

The second meaning of "centrality" allows identifying the node/agent with the highest capacity to arbitrate or intervene in the geodesic routes of the network, known as "the structural bridge". While in Figure 0 there are only 4 direct interactions registered, there are more geodesic routes, which are the paths that indirectly connect all the nodes/agents. For instance, there is a geodesic route connecting nodes/agents 2 and 3 through the node/agent 1, and there is another geodesic route connecting nodes/agents 2 and 4 also through node/agent 1, etc. Those geodesic routes –connecting nodes/agents 2 and 3, as well as nodes/agents 2 and 4– are the paths of information and other resources that flow and are indirectly distributed across the network.

After calculating the total amount of geodesic routes connecting the nodes/agents of the network, the *betweenness* indicator allows identifying the node/agent with the highest capacity to intervene in those geodesic routes. As observed in Figure 0, the node/agent 1 intervenes in every route of the network because there is not a single path connecting nodes/agents 2, 3, 4 and 5 that does not pass through node/agent 1; therefore, node/agent 1 registers a *betweenness* indicator of 100% which means that it has the highest capacity to intervene in the resources flowing across the network. In this case, node/agent 1 has the greatest capacity to decide, for instance, which pieces of information will be communicated to the other nodes/agents.

Lava Jato: Political Protection, Money Laundering and Millionaire Contracts

According to the judicial sources listed in Annex, this investigation began on March 17th, 2014, following a complaint filed by Hermes Freitas Magnus, who owned the company "Dunel" along with Maria Teodora Silva. In 2008, the owners of "Dunel" searched investors to capitalize their company, allowing former deputy José Janene to invest in it and to be included in its executive board. The former deputy took advantage of his position as an investor to launder money derived from corruption at Petrobras. Hermes Freitas and Maria Teodora Silva informed to authorities the suspicious operations taking place in their company, as well as their unjustified exclusion from Dunel's board due to their unconformity with the scheme adopted.

The investigation against José Janene and Alberto Youssef initially uncovered this illicit structure, revealing a corrupt system established to participate in public tenders for investment projects and to hire services at Petrobras. The scheme consisted of bribe payments paid by a group of companies referenced in the judicial sources as "The Club".

"The Club" was a cartel conformed by several companies that coordinated their own participation in Petrobras' projects, set prices for providing services and paying bribes. At the time of the meetings, the involved companies already knew which one would get a contract with Petrobras, although the selected one would fulfill the requirements during the public tender.

For instance, the construction company "Constructora Camargo Correa", directed by Dalton dos Santos, won one of the Petrobras biddings. To make effective the 1% bribe payment to Paulo Roberto Costa, a Petrobras high-ranking official, both parties simulated contracts to transfer money through the company "Costa Global", controlled by Paulo Roberto Costa. Additionally, "Constructora Camargo Correa" made agreements on its own with the companies "Sanko Sider" and "Sanko Servicos", which were presented as suppliers in its financial notes. The receipts and documents that were managed by the three companies presented overpriced supplies, a common strategy used to hide irregular payments.

In general, to obtain contracts and establish agreements, "The Club" paid between 1% and 3% of the value of every contract to Petrobras officials such as (i) Paulo Roberto Costa, former director of Supplies; (ii) Renato de Souza Duque, former director of Engineering Directorate and (iii) Pedro José Barusco, former Services manager. Bribes were also intended for political parties or agents, herein categorized as politicians, who in turn provided political support for nominating and keeping aforementioned directors in their positions. For instance, the supplies directorate at Petrobras was controlled by the *Partido Progressista Brasileiro*, (PP or PPB) [Brazilian Progress Party]; the engineering board, by the *Partido dos Trabalhadores*, PT [Workers Party]; and the international board, by the *Partido do Movimento Democrático Brasileiro*, PMDB [Brazilian Democratic Movement]. Some bribes were paid directly to members of the parties or to the party itself through offshore accounts, front companies or just delivering in cash.

Another strategy to deliver monetary bribes consisted of funding political campaigns of politicians and public officials. For instance, senators Jorge Afonso Argello, from the Brazilian Labor Party, PTB, requested undue payments from various companies involved in the illicit scheme of Petrobras and in exchange offered to protect those companies during investigations. The payments of those bribes were registered as electoral donations to the São Pedro Parish, in Tabatinga/DF. Later, the same Parish requested a payment of R$ 350,000 to the President of the Brazilian corporation OAS, José Adelmário Pinheiro Filho, who was told that Jorge Afonso Argello had a strong bond with that Parish and that "it was –politically– fundamental for him [Pinheiro Filho] to give that donation". The payments delivered by OAS totaled five million *reais*, approximately USD$ 1,495,573.

To conceal and manage large amounts of money without legal restrictions, Fernando Soares, Nestor Cerveró, Paulo Roberto Costa, Pedro José Barusco, Renato Duque, and Jorge Luiz Zelada, second director of Petrobras International Department, opened offshore accounts in Swiss banks and, from there, executed frequent financial transferences. Money resulting from those illicit transactions was transferred to accounts in Hong Kong, Virgin Islands, Mainland China, and Monaco, among other countries, in different currencies. The illicit scheme developed the strategy known as "dollar-cape", which consists of purchasing and selling foreign currencies through a compensation system: the foreign currency is delivered through a foreign deposit to a buyer in Brazil. This transaction implies an international transfer of money, similar to the one carried out by banks, but through an informal system, unregulated by the law. The operations in the black currencies market were executed by "*doleiros*" that had an essential role in money laundering, evasion of taxes related to the exchange of currencies and deliverance and transference of bribes.

Another strategy for money laundering consisted of transferring bribes through commodities and goods such as luxury apartments, cars, and paintings instead of money, to avoid tracking the sources and movements of bribes. Additionally, nodes/agents involved in the illicit network created and managed front companies that existed only on paper, without facilities or without providing real services or products. Third parties that established fraudulent contracts, owned those front companies to transfer massive amounts of money under the appearance of legality, therefore, evading controls by authorities. Another strategy to pay bribes consisted of establishing fraudulent debt agreements and loans between legal, front and offshore companies and financial institutions.

Some of the companies participating in "The Club" were: Construction company Camargo Correa, RNEST Refinery, Getúlio Vargas REPAR Refinery, Galvão Engenharia, Engevix, OAS, Odebrecht, Andrade, UTC, Queiroz Galvão, Promon, MPE, Techinit, GDCAR, and Mendes Júnior, among others. So far, in the context of the "Lava Jato" operation about 260 people have been accused under 56 criminal charges, while 130 individuals, including prominent politicians and businessmen, have been sentenced to jail in 29 judicial sentences.

According to data revealed by the Paraná prosecutor's office in charge of the main "Lava Jato" investigations, in southern Brazil, the number of bribes registered reached USD$ 2 billion, approximately R$ 6.4 billion. It is estimated, however, that the total damages to Petrobras for diversion of funds and overprices could even exceed USD$ 13 billion.[77]

---

77 The mentioned sources are available at: http://www.mpf.mp.br/para-o-cidad-ao/caso-lava-jato/atuacao-na-1a-instancia/parana/resultado

Approaching the Sub-structures

Media outlets across Latin America have extensively covered cases of corruption related to Odebrecht. However, other companies and illicit sub-structures briefly described below were also part of the entire "Lava Jato" structure.

Additionally, in Chapter 5, 6, 7 and 8, some of these sub-structures are analyzed in detail.

Eletronuclear

Under his collaborative agreement, Dalton Avancini, former president of Camargo Correa S.A., revealed the existence of an illicit structure operating within the state company Eletrobras Termonuclear S.A. – Eletronuclear. The illicit structure shared the *modus operandi* identified in Petrobras: alliances between companies to obtain undue advantages at State companies, payment of bribes to public officers, and money laundering. Due to the lifting of bank secrecy of companies Andrade Gutierrez and Engevix, also involved in the Petrobras scandal, authorities identified transferences to the former president of Eletronuclear, Othon Luiz, for contracts at Angra 3, a nuclear reactor project. According to the indictment, the representatives of Engevix, José Antunes and Cristiano Kok, executed 29 transferences to Othon Luiz.

The illicit scheme of money laundering operated through the financial movement resulting from contracts signed between Andrade Gutierrez and CG Impex. Other 5 contracts were simulated to transfer large amounts of money to

Othon Luiz, established between CG Impex and Aratec. The approximate value transferred through fraudulent contracts was of USD$ 628,979.51 (R$ 2,045,001.53) through 38 transactions.

J&F Group

The scheme of bribery and money laundering carried out by the J&F Group and its subsidiaries JBS, Eldorado, Florestal, and Vigor operated from 2003 to 2017. This illicit scheme illegitimately obtained public funds from the state bank "Banco Nacional de Desenvolvimiento Economico e Social", the "*Caixa Econômica Federal*" (CEF), the "*Fundação dos Economiários Federais*" (FUNCEF) and the "*Fundação Petrobras de Seguridade Social*" (PETROS), by supporting political campaigns and paying bribes to strategic political agents.

According to the investigation, the J&F Group, owned by Joesley Mendoça Batista and Wesley Mendoça Batista, supported the campaigns of candidates running for the Chamber of Representatives, the Senate, and the Directorate of public institutions. In fact, the Group funded the electoral campaigns of governors of 4 States during 16 periods, and the presidential campaigns of Dilma Rousseff and Michel Temer.

Brazilian prosecutors estimate that the total amount of bribes reached USD$ 184,541,574 (R$ 600,000,000.00) paid to 1829 political agents ascribed to 28 political parties. These transactions were executed through fraudulent invoices between the company JBS and other companies such as Grafica e Editora Alvorada Ltda, ST Pesquisa de Mercado Ltda EPP, Instituto Icone de Ensino Jurídico Ltda, IBOPE

Inteligéncia Pesquisa e Consultoria Ltda, Bartz Propaganda Ltda, among several others.

Sergio Cabral

The judicial operations Calicute and Eficiencia uncovered an illicit structure articulated by former governor Sergio Cabral. The structure participated in corruption and money laundering for more than USD$ 100 million, through transfers of assets abroad. It is known that Sergio Cabral requested a bribe rate of 5% of all administrative contracts with the State since the moment he took office as Chief Executive of the state of Rio de Janeiro on January 1, 2007.

To manage the mentioned bribery scheme, Sergio Cabral hired Renato Chebar, a financial market operator, to hide on his behalf the bribes he received in foreign bank accounts through dollar-cable. He also hired Carlos Bezerra to register all bribery incomes. According to the accounting records accumulated by operator Carlos Bezerra, it was identified that Marco Antonio de Luca, one of the active members of the scheme and manager of the company Masan Servicios Especializados Ltda., contributed at least with an amount reaching R$ 12,595,700.00 (USD$ 3,956,000) for briberies in kind, in favor of the company ORCRIM, controlled by Sergio Cabral, related to contracts signed with the State of Rio de Janeiro.

The complaint submitted by the Public Prosecutor's Office under the Calicute Operation identified active and passive corruption and subsequent assets laundering around contracts signed between the Rio de Janeiro State and companies Andrade Gutierrez, Delta, Carioca Engenharia, Oas, Queiroz Galvao, Camargo Correa, Camter,

Eit, and Odebrecht. Two cases were particularly prominent among this illicit scheme articulated by Sergio Cabral: the fraud in a public tender for the promised restoration for the *Maracaná* Stadium and the fraud in public tenders for Cap Favelas works, both between 2007 and 2009. Both cases are discussed below.

Odebrecht

The case of the company Odebrecht has been perhaps the most popular and covered by media across Latin America. By November 2014, when the Federal Police of Brazil unveiled "The Club", Odebrecht had 19 contracts with Petrobras, for approximately R$ 17 billion (USD$ 5,084,949).

In June 2015, Marcelo Odebrecht, the legal owner of the company, was arrested and the Judge Sergio Moro sentenced him to 19 years in prison under charges of corruption, money laundering and criminal conspiracy. In March 2016, it was revealed that Odebrecht replicated the similar money laundering and corruption scheme that established with Petrobras, in ten Latin American and two Africans countries, totaling USD$ 785 million in bribes paid since 2001.[78] In general, as it discussed in the following chapters, Odebrecht participated in several illicit operations related to infrastructure across the sub-structures analyzed. This means that there is not a single chapter dedicated to Odebrecht because this company intervened in most of the analyzed sub-networks.

---

78 Folha de Sao Paulo (Dec 22, 2016) "Odebrecht group paid Out US$ 1 billion bribes in 12 countries, says USA. Source: https://www1.folha.uol.com.br/internacional/en/brazil/2016/12/1843856-odebrecht-group-paid-out-us-1-billion-in-bribes-in-12-countries-says-usa.shtml

The case of the company Odebrecht is useful to understand the scope of "Lava Jato". Although this company is just one of several others involved in the entire network of macro-corruption it is probably the most relevant one. As it can be observed in Figure 1 below, the sub-structure of corruption established by Odebrecht (darker node/ agent) is so massive that its interactions (darker lines) affect several areas of the "Lava Jato" overall network.

Figure 1. The Odebrecht node/agent and interactions of the Odebrecht sub-network in darker color.

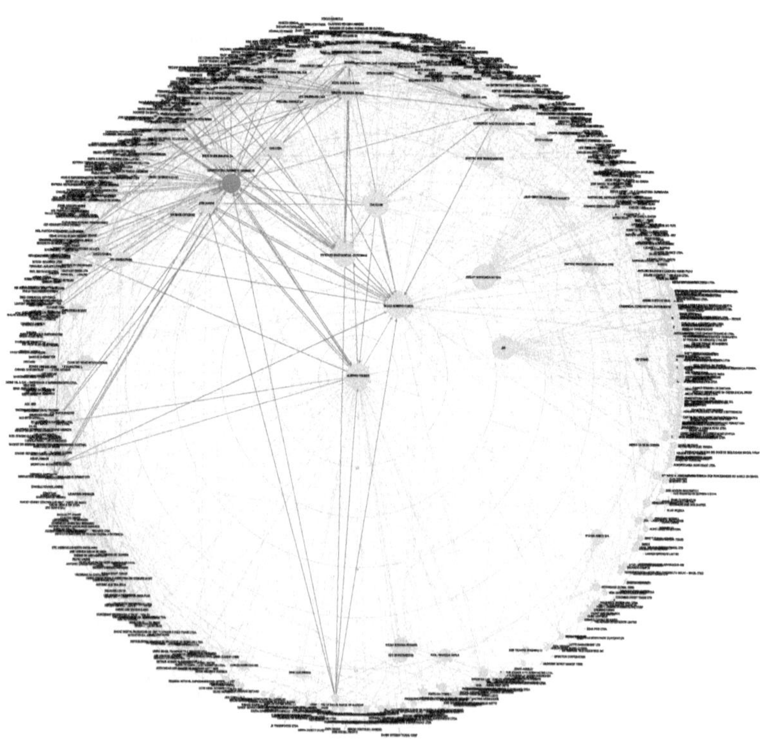

However, the real scope of Odebrecht is revealed when its sub-networks is moved outside of the "Lava Jato" structure, as illustrated below. Hundreds of indirect interactions established through the nodes/agents Petrobras, Alberto Youseff and Pablo Roberto Costa, allowed Odebrecht to reach a large area of the entire "Lava Jato" network. In fact, the overall "Lava Jato" structure loses its nucleus (Alberto Youseff) when the Odebrecht sub-network is moved out; therefore, this sub-network affects the "Lava Jato" structure with a group of only 41 nodes/agents and 103 direct interactions (Figure 2).

Figure 2. The Odebrecht sub-network outside of the "Lava Jato" structure.

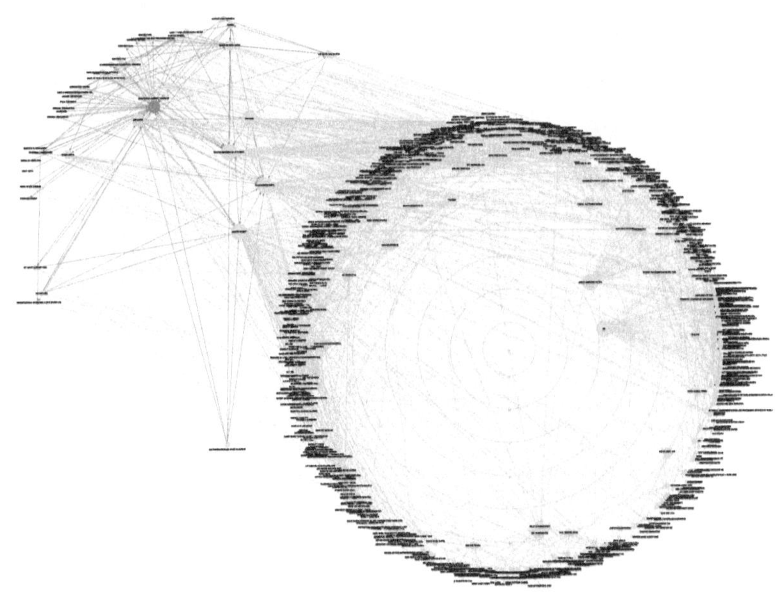

Analyzed Sources

In order to elaborate the models herein analyzed, court decisions extracted from four police operations at the first instance of investigation were processed through the methodology and protocols previously described: Lava Jato, Dolce Vita, Bidone and Casablanca, each one focused on an illicit organization run by the defendants Carlos Habib Chater, Alberto Youseff, Nelma Kodama and Henrique Srour. Decisions were executed by the Federal Police on March 17th and 24th, 2014. Then, in the second stage of analysis, 29 sentences between 2014 and 2016, at the first and second instances of investigation of the Lava Jato Operation were processed and analyzed.[79]

Judicial sentences were gathered and analyzed instead of complaints since the information collected at the beginning of the investigation was confirmed or denied during the prosecution; therefore, the sentences convey more reliable information. During the third stage of the present analysis, the information of the sentences was complemented with data sustained on court decisions and annexes of judicial processes extracted from the websites hhtps://jota.info/lavajota/ and http://lavajato.mpf.mp.br/. Those annexes were also used to detail the sub-structures of the Lava Jato Operation.

---

79 The mentioned sources are available at: http://lavajato.mpf.mp.br/atuacao-na-1a-instancia/denuncias-do-mpf

Chapter 4. The Macro-Corruption Network

Nodes/agents

After processing the sources above mentioned, a total of 906 nodes/agents were identified, categorized as Private (65%), Public (19%), Criminal (11%), and Other (5%).

Private Players

The most relevant type of nodes/agents groups members of the private sector: 65% out of the total number of nodes/agents (Table 1). Most nodes/agents grouped under this category are Brazilian corporations (252) and businesspersons (170) involved in the scheme, paying bribes to obtain undue privileges to contract with the State. This category also includes offshore companies (109) used by the participants of the illicit network to obtain fraudulent contracts and, through those agreements, pay bribes to public servants, politicians, and political parties.

A total of 21 Brazilian Consortiums created by legit and façade companies to achieve undue advantages in public contracts were also grouped under this category, with 15 offshore accounts, usually managed by third parties, that were essential to execute fraudulent transactions, since Brazilian authorities lacked jurisdiction to follow the movements of these accounts and, therefore, it was impossible to effectively track the origin or destination of the deposited funds.

"Construtora Norberto Odebrecht" was one of the Brazilian companies most involved in this illicit scheme. To pay bribes between December 2006 and June 2014, the company executed financial transferences abroad through offshore companies such as Smith & Nash Engineering Company, Arcadex Corporation, and Havinsur S.A., to pay bribes to Petrobras officials in accounts such as Sagar Holdings and Quinus Service, both controlled by Paulo Roberto Costa, Milzart Overseas, controlled by Renato Duque, and Pexo Corporation, controlled by Pedro Barusco.

Table 1. Nodes/Agents classified as Private. "Lava Jato" Network.

Private – Brazilian Company	252
Private – Businessperson	170
Private – Offshore Company	109
Private – Brazilian Consortium	21
Private – offshore account	15
Private – Facade Company	12
Private – Lawyer	10
Private – Money Carrier	7
Private – Pension Fund	4
Private – Brazilian Institution	2
Private – Advertising agent	3
Private – Civil Association	1
Private – Journalist	1
Private – Political adviser	1
Total	608

The "Private" category also includes 12 front companies that were created to legalize financial transactions. For instance, Mo Consultoria was a company created and controlled by Alberto Yousseff, that did not offer real products or services but that was used to sign several fraudulent contracts with Petrobras, Sanko Sider e Sanko Servicios, Consórcio Rnest – Conest, Galvão Engenharia S.A., Consórcio SEHAB Ltda., and OAS Ltda., among other companies. These companies transferred to MO Consultoria approximately USD$ 795,233 between 2009 and 2013, aimed at the payment of bribes.

The remaining "Private" nodes/agents include various professionals who provided legal or political advice, paid bribes, served as third parties to conceal the source of bribes, hid evidence or participated in meetings to decide what company should receive a given public contract.

Public Players

The "Public" category (19%), distributed as shown in Table 2, groups 100 civil servants and 24 former members of the Chamber of Deputies with political influence to nominate delegates for Petrobras directories. Some of them also coordinated underground meetings with investigated companies that were favored with public contracts.

This category also groups 16 Brazilian politicians such as José Dirceu de Oliveira e Silva and João Luiz Argolo, both of them charged under passive corruption; 13 political parties such as *Partido da Mobilização Nacional* (PMN), *Partido dos Trabalhadores* (PT), and *Partido da República*, among others; 9 Eletronuclear officials; 8 Public institutions involved in corruption; and 7 Petrobras officials mainly in charge of acquiring supplies, coordinating engineering services and arranging international hiring of other companies, such as Paulo Roberto Costa, Pedro Barusco and Celso Araripe de Oliveira.

Table 2. Nodes/agents classified as Public officials. "Lava Jato" Network.

Public – Civil servant	100
Public – Federal Deputy	24
Public – Brazilian Politician	16
Public – Political Party	13
Public – Eletronuclear functionary	9
Public – Government institution	8
Public – Petrobras functionary	7
Public – Petrobras Area	3
Public – Brazilian Energy Company	2
Public – Former President of Brazil	2
Public – Public trust	2
Public – Brazilian Ministry	2
Public – Federal Government	1
Public – Ministers	1
Public – Federal Prosecutor	1
Public – President of Brazil	1
Public – Brazilian refinery	1
Total	193

The public officers involved in the scheme received bribe payments of 1% or 2% of the value of each contract that was fraudulently and unfairly assigned to specific companies. Additionally, 60% of the paid bribes were used to fund political parties and certain political campaigns. Although most nodes/agents participating in this illicit network are not public officers, their involvement was critical to sustain and articulate the corruption scheme.

Criminals

The category "Criminal" (11%) groups those nodes/agents carrying out criminal and illicit actions in the scheme. Although not all of them can be labeled as unlawful agents or "full-time" criminals, their role in the network can be defined as strictly illegal. This category specifically includes 47 third parties who provided their representation of accounts and companies to protect the real beneficiaries of transactions; 19 *doleiros* or intermediaries, such as Alberto Youssef and Nelma Kodama, who arranged meetings between companies, advised individuals and officials on the creation of offshore companies, and controlled front companies to legalize payments, among other tasks related to the currencies black market. Also, 9 bribe operators oversaw bribe payments among the participants of the illicit network.

The "Criminal" category also includes 8 drug traffickers who laundered their profits through the network, 7 accomplices of money laundering, 5 money launderers, and 3 illicit associations between legal companies and consortiums, such as "The Club", established to obtain undue advantages or to commit fraud through financial crimes and corruption (Table 3).

Other Players

The category "Other" groups (i) banks in which financial transactions were carried out, (ii) an unknown depositor of one of the offshore accounts, (iii) an investment fund and a financial institution used to transfer a loan agreement to launder money and pay bribes, and (v) an art collector (Table 4).

**Table 3. Nodes/agents classified as "Criminal".
"Lava Jato" Network.**

Third party	47
Doleiro – Intermediary	19
Bribe operator	9
Criminal – Drug Trafficker	8
Accomplice of money laundering	7
Criminal – Money Launderer	5
Cartel – Illicit association between companies	3
Total	98

**Table 4. Nodes/agents classified as "Other".
"Lava Jato" Network.**

Bank	3
Unknown Depositor	1
Investment Fund	1
Financial institution	1
Art collector	1
Total	7

Interactions

A total of 2,693 interactions were registered and modeled, distributed under the following categories: economic (48%), logistic (34%), other (11%), and political (7%).

The category consisting of "Economic" interactions (Table 5) groups 48% of all the interactions. Some of the main sub-categories within the "economic" interactions are: (i) "making financial transactions", with 676 interactions; (ii) "paying bribes or undue commissions", with 330 interactions; (iii) "money laundering", with 107 cases, and (iv) "simulation of contracts", with 105 interactions (Table

5). These interactions refer to the main financial operations needed to sustain the corruption scheme.

Among the main sub-categories other economic interactions were: (v) "being business partners", with 41 interactions, (vi) "paying an undue commission to establish contracts", with 22 interactions; (vii) "opening and controlling accounts of front companies", with 13 interactions, (viii) "capital investment in", with 10 interactions, (iv) "misappropriation of funds of", with 7 interactions that illustrate the illicit appropriation of money from companies or public funds, that then was invested to create front companies and to pay bribes, such as the case in which the firm Sete Brasil was constituted in part with the investment of misappropriated Petrobras funds and pension funds such as Petros, Previ, Funcef and Valia.

Table 5. "Economic" Interactions. "Lava Jato" Network.

Economic – Financial transactions to	676
Economic – Bribe payment to	330
Economic – Money laundering through	107
Economic – Simulating contracts with	105
Economic – Being business partners with	41
Economic – Paying an undue commission to establish contract with	22
Economic – Open and controlling offshore accounts on behalf of	13
Economic – Capital investment in	10
Economic – Misappropriation of funds of	7
Economic – Fraudulent Currency Exchange Operation through	6
Economic – Engaging in a Debt Agreement with	6
Economic – Paying debt with paintings to	1
Economic – Purchasing Paintings from	1
Total	1325

Other "Economic" interactions include "fraudulent currency exchange operations", with 6 cases of "dollar-cape" operations in which currencies are exchanged through informal channels to launder money, evade taxes, and keep the flows of money untraceable. Another sub-category was "engaging in a debt agreement", with 6 cases that exposed strategies used to deliver money through an apparently legal procedure. For instance, Salim Taufic Schahin, Milton Taufic Schahin and Fernando Schahin, owners and executives of the Schahin Group, delivered a bribe destined to Eduardo Musa and the Workers Party, PT, paid by for the concession, renewal and fraudulent discharge of a loan legally granted to José Carlos Bumlai, third party of the real final beneficiaries.

The category "Logistic" (Table 6) groups 964 logistic interactions that guaranteed the stability of the illicit network during its operation between 2009 and 2014. Some of the most relevant logistic sub-categories were: (i) "participating in the administrative board of a company", with 158 interactions; (ii) "being part of", with 75 interactions that refer to those cases in which contracts with Brazilian state companies were established through consortiums; (iii) "serving as third party to", with 132 interactions grouping those individuals that agreed to open an account or appear as legal representative of a company to hide its real beneficiaries, (iv) "decision-making and leadership (*de facto*) of", with 118 interactions that revealed the true beneficiaries of accounts, companies and properties that had an undefined or false titular; (v) "modification of an established contract", with 67 interactions that also revealed strategies of companies to push an unjustified increase of costs and extension of timeframe of infrastructure works initially arranged in contracts; (vi) "planning financial distribution", with 43 interactions of specific meetings in which it was decided the distribution of resources among the participants of the corrupt scheme.

Table 6. "Logistic" interactions. "Lava Jato" Network.

Logistic - Participating in the administrative, finances, chair, among other management positions	158
Logistic - Being part of	152
Logistic - Serving as third party to	132
Logistic - Decision-making and leadership (de facto) of	118
Logistic - Modification of a established contract with	67
Logistic- Planning financial distribution with	43
Logistic - Being the representative of	39
Logistic - Supporting fraudulent accounting	37
Logistic - Serving as intermediary of	35
Logistic - Had a business meeting with	32
Logistic - Legal Ownership of Company	32
Logistic - using companies to commit fraud	30
Logistic - Delivering money to	26
Logistic - Interfere with the course of justice for	18
Logistic - Influence on	16
Logistic - Providing legal advice to	8
Logistic - being a subsidiary company of	8
Logistic - Criminal - Dealt a drug delivery	5
Logistic - Acquiring names and personal information of third actors (used for fraudulent exchange operations) for	3
Logistic - Excluded illicitly from company	2
Logistic - Forgiving loan agreement to	1
Logistic - Transposing loan agreement to	1
Logistic - Criminal - Supplying illegal drugs to	1
Total	964

Other relevant logistic sub-categories are: (vii) "being the representative of", with 39 cases in which business-persons represented cartelized companies during arranged meetings; (viii) "supporting fraudulent accounting", with 37 interactions, revealing the accounting arrangements made to hide irregular monetary incomes and justify "artificial" expenses. "Legal ownership of company" (32 interactions); "Serving as intermediary of" (35 interactions) and describing the situation of "A person asking for a bribe payment or an irregular donation to a campaign in behalf of someone else", among other listed in Table 6.

As stated above, the "Lava Jato" Network operated though cartelized companies that obtained public contracts through undue advantage, paying 1% or 2% of the value of the contract to officials and political parties. To complete the payment of bribes, the main companies used small, façade and offshore companies, as well as offshore accounts. To carry the operations, launder money and hide evidence of the illicit structure, bribe operators, *doleiros*, third parties, intermediaries, and money carriers were hired.

The third category of interactions is "other" (11%), which includes sub-categories such as (i) the "establishment of contracts with State companies or institutions", with 124 cases, (ii) "networking", with 68 interactions that describe informal links with key nodes/agents of the network, (iii) "being a family member", with 28 interactions that describe family ties within the network, and (iv) "executing threads and pressure to commit financial crimes", with 4 interactions that describe coercion usually perpetrated by intermediaries or "*doleiros*" against other nodes/agents (Table 7).

Table 7. "Other" Interactions. "Lava Jato" Network.

State- Establishing contracts with	124
Networking	68
Family – Being a family member of	28
Violence – Threats and pressure to commit financial crimes	4

The fourth category of interactions groups the "political" operations (Table 8) in sub-categories such as (i) "benefiting particular interests of", with 76 cases in which a political agent benefits another node/agent through a particular decision or investment, (ii) 34 interactions consisting of "irregular donations to" political campaigns, (iii) 25 cases of "official donations to" fund political campaigns, (iv) 13 interactions "providing political favors to" specific nodes/agents, (v) "nominate for public office", with 5 interactions, and (vi) "providing political advice to", with 2 cases.

Table 8. "Political" Interactions. "Lava Jato" Network.

Political – Benefiting particular interest of	76
Political – Irregular donations (political campaign) to	34
Political – Official donations (political campaign) to	25
Political – Financing political campaign of	25
Political – Providing political favors to	13
Political – Nominated for public office	5
Political – Providing political advice to	2
Total	180

As it was explained in the description of the case, political parties and public officials received undue commissions paid by businesspersons to nominate Petrobras officials or to sustain them on their positions. Paulo Roberto Costa, for instance, declared on trial that when he was appointed as Director of Supplies at Petrobras, he met with José Janene, the former deputy responsible of his nomination, who requested Paulo Roberto Costa to use his influence to provide an undue advantage to "The Club" members on obtaining contracts with Petrobras. In fact, José Janene told Paulo Roberto Costa that he had to pay those bribes as a political favor to the political party, and as a result, the party would support him and, therefore, Paulo Roberto Costa would keep his position at Petrobras.

Arbitration of Resources

As stated in the methodological description, the *betweenness* indicator informs about those nodes/agents with the highest capacity to intervene in the indirect routes of the network. In this case, the nodes/agents with the highest *betweenness* indicators were (i) Alberto Yousseff with 9.4%, (ii) the Petrobras company itself, intervening in 9.4% of the geodesic routes, (iii) Paulo Roberto Costa, a Petrobras official, with an indicator of 4.9%, and (iv) the company JBS, with 3.7% (Figure 3).

The following agents with the highest *betweenness* indicator were: (v) Joesley Mendonca Batista (JB), responsible of JBS's expansion and internationalization, with an indicator of 3.3%; (vi) "The Club", referring to those cartelized companies that co-opted the contracting process at Petrobras, Eletrobras, and Eletronuclear, with 3.3%; (vii) Julio Gerin de Almeida Camargo, one of the bribing operators of the network, with 3.1%, and (viii) Pedro Barusco, a Petrobras official, with 3%.

These eight nodes/agents with the highest *betweenness* indicators intervene in 40.1% of the geodesic routes –or indirect paths of the network–, which means that this group of individuals and companies had the greatest capacity to arbitrate and distribute resources such as information and money among the participants. Removing some of those node/agents would modify the structure of the network because Petrobras, for instance, was the main company in which the corruption took place and, therefore, it was involved in most of the economic and logistic interactions.

In the same sense, Alberto Youssef was a key agent on stabilizing the illicit network, since he was in charge of advising businesspersons and public officials about the necessary operations to guarantee the ongoing operation of the network, while coordinating with other intermediaries and *doleiros* the strategies to launder money and to deliver bribe payments; strategies such as establishing alliances between businesspersons and public officials with political power, creating and handling offshore accounts or companies to conduct illicit financial transactions, or taking advantage of the currencies black market to evade taxes, resulted of the support that Alberto Youssef provided.

The medium to high concentration of the *betweenness* indicator suggests that the network has a relatively medium to low level of resilience, since isolating or removing near 8 key nodes/agents, in the case of Petrobras, that represent just the 0.44% of the total amount of nodes/agents, would drastically affect the structure of the network.

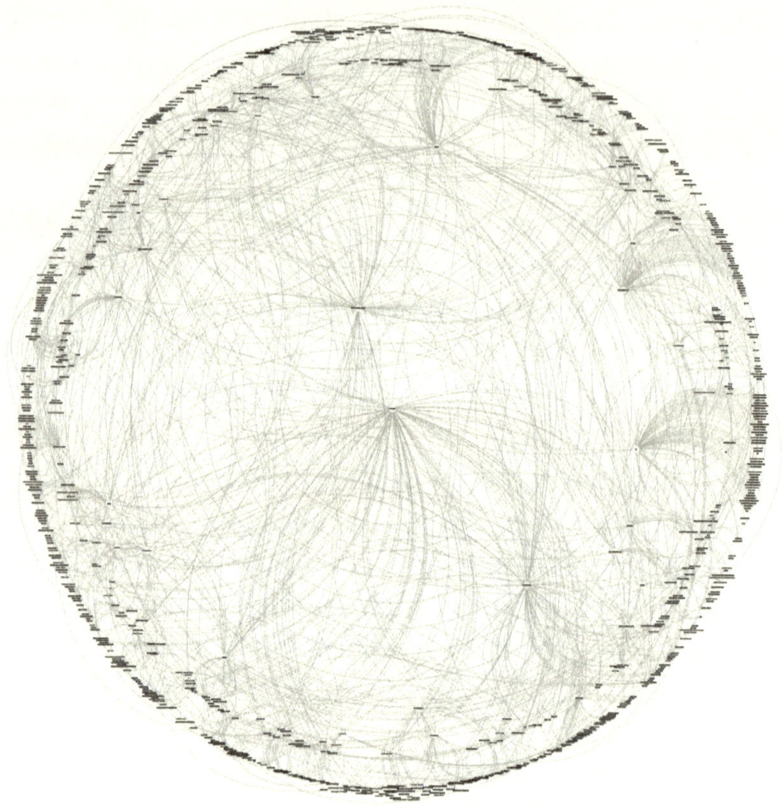

Figure 3. *Betweenness* **indicators of the "Lava Jato" Network. Size and location of the nodes/agents represent the indicator of** *betweenness* **(capacity to arbitrate resources across the network).**

Direct Centrality

The four nodes/agents with the highest degree of "direct individual centrality" are: (i) Alberto Youssef, with an indicator of 3.4%, acting as an operator in the financial black market and coordinating financial operations of the illicit network, (iii) Paulo Roberto Costa, with an indicator of 2.6%, as a Petrobras official with a vast amount of direct interactions registered, mainly paying bribes, (ii) Petrobras, as the hub company where the corruption scheme is focused, with an indicator of 2.2%, and (iv) JBS, with an indicator of

1.9%, as the company involved in several licit and illicit transactions such as simulated public contract (Figure 4).

Other nodes/agents with a high direct centrality level were: (v) Joesley Mendonca Batista, one of the administrative managers of JBS, with an indicator of 1.8%; (vi) "The Clube" as a *cliqué* of companies with a high capacity of interaction to obtain advantages on Petrobras contracts, with an indicator of 1.7%; (vii) Constructora Norberto Odebrecht, the company that replicated the Petrobras illicit scheme and paid bribes to high-ranking officials in 12 countries, with an indicator of 1.1%, and (viii) Jose Janene, a former federal deputy in charge of controlling an important part of the bribery scheme of the illicit network, who registered an indicator of 1.1%.

Alberto Youssef, Petrobras and Paulo Roberto Acosta are not only the nodes/agents with the highest indicator of direct centrality in the network, but also the nodes/agents with the highest capacity for intervening and arbitrating resources across the network. Therefore, these nodes/agents had a critical role in stabilizing the network.

Additionally, the first eight nodes/agents with the highest indicators of direct centrality, which represent just the 0.88% of the total amount of nodes/agents, concentrate 29.4% of the total direct interactions of the network. Interesting enough, the remaining nodes/agents have a direct centrality indicator between 0.1% up to 1.1%.

Figure 4. Direct Centrality of the "Lava Jato" Illicit Network. Size and location of the nodes represent the indicator of direct centrality.

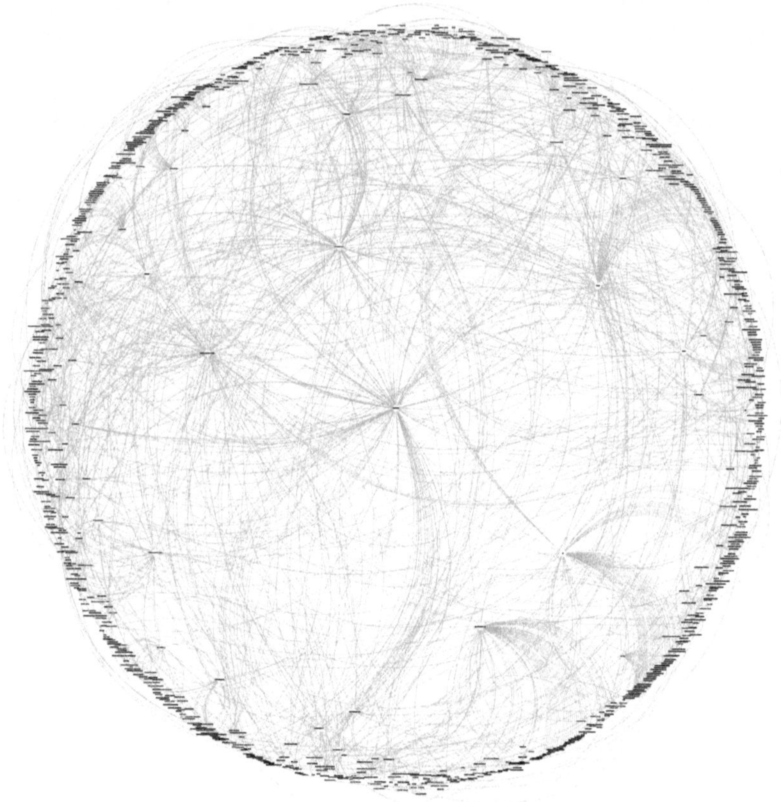

Resilience

The high level of both the concentration of direct centrality and the *betweenness* indicator in around 8 nodes/agents (less than 1% of total agents of the illicit network) reflects an illicit structure with a relatively medium to medium-low level of resilience regarding direct interactions. However, in practice, the level of resilience could be lower than the suggested by indicators due to the central role played by Petrobras in this illicit network, utilized to pursue illicit purposes by some of their directors. A decisive countervailing factor that tends to strengthen its resilience is the variety of distinctive sub-networks, illustrated and discussed in the next chapter, that conglomerate in the analyzed illicit network as a whole.

The most outstanding characteristic of the "Lava Jato" network is perhaps the variety of powerful sub-networks around key private companies and state entities conglomerated to co-opt state institutions and to strategically develop and reproduce a macro-corruption system in Brazil under a transnational scope of reference. Bearing that in mind, the following chapter and annexes are dedicated to analyze the most important sub-networks' operation.

Chapter 5. The Petrobras Sub-network

Introduction

Before analyzing the main sub-networks in the following chapters, it is important to bear in mind that the facts and analysis discussed herein are sustained on records released by the Brazilian Public Ministry, which informs about the various stages of the judicial operation included in the entire "Lava Jato" operation. Several names and events are discussed to understand the intricate details of the illicit operation, and those names were extracted from the extended list of judicial documents listed in the Annex. It is also important to highlight that the presumption of innocence, in observance of individual rights, is always preserved regarding the names quoted and referenced in this book and, especially, in this and the following four chapter. This means that changes in the sentences as result of appeals would modify the characteristics of the model herein discussed. As stated at the beginning of this book, the judicial truth is the jurisdiction of the courts, which by law will decide whether the mentioned defendants are innocent or guilty.

In the case of ongoing investigations, definitive judicial sentences will clarify the penal responsibility of each node/ agent involved in the illicit structures herein analyzed;

that is why each judicial source is referenced in the following analysis. At this point it is worth to stress that the commission of criminal acts form the legal perspective strictly corresponds to the judicial truth, which is less comprehensive than the social and historical truth due to the limitations that the formal legal framework imposes when some actions are not penalized by the prevailing law but are subject of moral rejection due to their perverse social impacts.

Bearing this in mind, in this and the following three chapters, key sub-networks of the "Lava Jato" structure are analyzed, focusing attention in the most relevant nodes/ agents and the most important carried out operations. The analysis begins with this Chapter, in which the Petrobras sub-network is analyzed; then, in Chapter 6, the Eletrobras – Eletronuclear sub-network; in Chapter 7, the Sergio Cabral sub-network; and in Chapter 8 the J&F Group sub-network. On one hand, the first and the second sub-networks illustrate how cartelized companies, such as "The Club", that paid bribes to key officials and political agents to access undue advantages in public contracts with Petrobras, replicated their illicit operations to obtain contracts or to manipulate bidding processes with the company Eletrobras – Eletronuclear and the Government of Rio de Janeiro. On the other hand, the Sergio Cabral and the J&F Group sub-networks unveil a criminal scheme sustained in the involvement of high-level politicians, including two former presidents and the current Brazilian president, political parties and civil servants who used their positions to seek strategies to defraud Brazilian public administration, hand by hand with powerful private companies and agents.

Paulo Roberto da Costa

Paulo Roberto da Acosta began his career in Petrobras in 1977 holding several managerial and technical positions. In 2004, the *Partido Progresista* (PP), which at the time was directed by Jose Janene, sponsored him to take on the Supplying Management position.[80] In return for the support, Paulo Roberto Costa provided undue advantages during the bidding processes with Petrobras, to companies linked with the political party.

Accordingly, once Paulo Roberto da Costa was appointed as Manager of Supplies in Petrobras, under the guidance of the *Partudo Progressista*, he returned the favors not only to the PP itself but also to the *Partido de Movimento Democrático Brasileiro* (PMDB), the *Partido da Social Democracia Brasileira* (PSDB), and the *Partido dos Trabhaladores* by facilitating access to Petrobras' contracts and resources[81]. As an illustrative example: The negotiation in 2010 with the *Partido da Social Democracia Brasileira* (PSDB) in exchange for bailing the establishment of the *Comissão Parlamentar de Inquérito* (CPI) that year.[82]

In 2006, Alberto Youssef became Paulo Roberto's financial operator to complete the transactions between companies of "The Clube" and the *Partido Progressista* (PP)[83]. To coordinate the bribe percentages and the details related to the bidding processes, directors of the "The Clube" companies met regularly with Petrobras functionaries.

---

80 Policia Federal Superintendência Regional No Estado Do Paraná, Delegacia Regional de Combate ao Crime Organizado e Delegacia de Repressão a Crimines contra o Sistema Financeiro e Desvio de Verbas Publicas. (2014). *Termo de Colaboração No. 01 Termo de Declarações que presta PAULO ROBERTO COSTA.* Page 2.
81 Ibid.
82 Ibid.
83 Ibid. Page 4.

Some of the multinational corporations participating in this illicit/criminal scheme were Oas, Galvao Ingenieria, Engevix, Iesa, Camargo Correa, Utc, Odebrecht, Mendez Junion, Setal, Mitsui Toyo, Skankas, Queiroz Galvao, Andrade Gutierrez, and Tome Ingenieria; as well as mid-size companies such as Jaragua Equipamentos, Construcap, Engesa, Delta, and Toshiba.[84]

By the same year, 2006, a political movement emerged from some Petrobras' officials with the purpose of dismissing Paulo Roberto Costa from the Supplying Management. To prevent this, the parliamentary group of the *Partido do Movimento Democrático Brasileiro* (PMDB) appeared in the scene with politicians such as Valdir Raupp, Renan Calheiros, Romero Juca, and the Minister Edson Lobao. Since that moment, *the Partido do Movimento Democrático Brasileiro* (PMDB) received a fraction of the bribes related to Petrobras' contracts, using Fernando Soares' services as a financial operator to transfer assets to the *Partido do Movimento Democrático Brasileiro* (PMDB).[85]

To understand the *modus operandi* of this illicit network, it is essential to understand the granting contracts process: before opening a bidding, the Petrobras' Research Center (CENPES)[86] designs a basic engineering project[87], and then the Budgetary Commission calculates a reference budget,

---

84 Policia Federal Superintendência Regional No Estado Do Paraná, Delegacia Regional de Combate ao Crime Organizado e Delegacia de Repressão a Crimines contra o Sistema Financeiro e Desvio de Verbas Publicas. (2014). *Termo de Colaboração No. 01 Termo de Declarações que presta ALBERTO YOUSSEF.* Page 3.
85 Ibid. Page 4.
86 From its Portuguese initials.
87 Policia Federal Superintendência Regional No Estado Do Paraná, Delegacia Regional de Combate ao Crime Organizado e Delegacia de Repressão a Crimines contra o Sistema Financeiro e Desvio de Verbas Publicas. (2014). *Termo de Colaboração No. 02 Termo de Declarações que presta PAULO ROBERTO COSTA.* Page 2.

defining a market price range, social charges, Bonus Rates (BDI)[88], and direct costs. Additional to this Budgetary Commission, there is a Tender Board for each project; however, the Tender Board does not elaborate a reference budget, instead, it verifies Petrobras' records for companies with a Certificate of Cadastral Enrollment (CRCC)[89], to define which companies are suitable to participate in the bidding. In this stage, on certain occasions, the companies pay a bribe to the Management Services for obtaining an invitation to participate in the bidding process.[90]

In this specific case, it was through a Bonus Rate that the companies concretized the bidding fraud: Three elements define the BDI: the profits of the project, related to the risks of executing the project, and the indirect costs that cannot be defined at the beginning but that are important for executing the project.[91] The third element - indirect costs or expenses- can be grouped as (i) local and central administrative, (ii) commercial, (iii) financial, and (iv) fiscal. Thus, the BDI is the sum of the components described above, expressed as a percentage of direct costs, which in the end is used for defining the price for the work.[92]

Each company had its own approach to modify the BDI, but these modifications usually varied between 10% and 20% of the project, although "The Clube" companies often exceeded this percentage.[93] In this case, the constructors

---

88 From its Portuguese initials.
89 From its Portuguese initials.
90 Policia Federal Superintendência Regional No Estado Do Paraná, Delegacia Regional de Combate ao Crime Organizado e Delegacia de Repressão a Crimines contra o Sistema Financeiro e Desvio de Verbas Publicas. (2014). *Termo de Colaboração No. 02 Termo de Declarações que presta PAULO ROBERTO COSTA.* Page 2.
91 Ibid.
92 Ibid. Page 3.
93Ibid.

or consortiums that Petrobras recruited, altered the BDI by including costs that didn't exist or quantities that didn't coincide with the market's reference.[94] Thus, the winning company charged extra for the costs of the project, which increased significantly the initial price of the project until reaching the amount required for covering the costs of the bribes, plus a profit. In general, the bribes were paid to political parties, to Petrobras' official, and to financial operators, after modifying the BDI section.[95]

Thus, if the companies didn't produce the extra costs and the subsequent profit required for paying the bribes to the political group, they were excluded of the biddings and the execution of their projects was obstructed.[96] As a result, the procedures and the extra costs were "institutionalized" and, therefore, applied to every project that Petrobras and other public entities required. In fact, the procedure for diverting public resources became permanent to favor the political group that dominated each particular economic sector or each position in the public companies.[97]

The average percentage paid as bribe to the political groups was 3% of the total value of the contract, but sometimes it decreased to 2% or increased to 15%, depending on each project.[98] Regarding the sponsored managements by the *Partido dos Trabhaladores* (PT), the percentage was aimed directly at the party by Jose Vaccari, the Party's treasurer.[99]

---

94 Ibid.

95 Policia Federal Superintendência Regional No Estado Do Paraná, Delegacia Regional de Combate ao Crime Organizado e Delegacia de Repressão a Crimines contra o Sistema Financeiro e Desvio de Verbas Publicas. (2014). *Termo de Colaboração No. 01 Termo de Declarações que presta Paulo Roberto Costa.* Page 4.

96 Ibid.

97 Ibid.

98 Ibid.

99 Ibid.

Each contractor had its own mechanism for delivering the bribe to the corresponding political group. In the specific case of the Supplying Management, 2% was delivered to the *Partido dos Trabhaladores* transferred directly to Jose Vaccari, and 1% was delivered to the *Partido Progressista*, and even sometimes divided between the *Partido dos Trabhaladores*, the *Partido de Movimento Democrático Brasileiro* (PMDB) and once with the *Partido da Social Democracia Brasileira* (PMDB)[100]. Regarding the 1% paid to the *Partido Progressista*, it was distributed as follows: 25% was deducted from charges made for issuing invoices and transportation, and the remaining was divided in 5% for Alberto Youssef, 5% for Joào Claudio Genu, 60% for Jose Janene, and 30% for Paulo Roberto Costa.[101] Following this procedure, money was carried in cash *by* and *to* Alberto Youssef, through emissaries such as Rafael Ángulo Lopez, Adarlco Negromonte, and Jaime a.k.a. "Careca". The amount of money delivered oscillated between R$ 200 thousand and R$ 300 thousand in each opportunity.[102]

Now, to provide a legal appearance to the financial transfers relative to bribes, a billing or deposit system was used, as in the case of Odebrecht[103]. Jose Janene managed the parallel and illegal accounting control until 2010, and subsequently Alberto Youssef, Joào Claudio Genu, and Paulo Roberto Costa. Off-shore accounts belonging to Leonardo Mirelles, Nelma Penasso, Carlos Rocha, and Vulgo Ceara were used for transferring money to foreign

---

100 Ibid.
101 Ibid.
102 Ibid.
103 Policia Federal Superintendência Regional No Estado Do Paraná, Delegacia Regional de Combate ao Crime Organizado e Delegacia de Repressão a Crimines contra o Sistema Financeiro e Desvio de Verbas Publicas. (2014). *Termo de Colaboração No. 01 Termo de Declarações que presta Alberto Youssef.* Page 4.

accounts. For moving cash, transactions were simulated through the companies: MO Consultoria, RCI Informatica, Empreiteira Rigidez, Labogem, Petroquimica, Hmar, and KFC Hidrossemeadura, among others, under the name of Waldomiro de Oliveira and Leonardo Mirelles. In exchange for using their companies, Waldomiro de Oliveira and Leonardo Mirelles obtained 14.5% of the operational designated cost, 25% of the 1% destined to the PP, and it was their responsibility to pay the resulting taxes.[104]

After Paulo Roberto Costa's departure from the Supplying Management, the payments for the contracts approved under the Paulo's administration were arranged as follows: 70% to Paulo Roberto, 15% to Alberto Youssef, and 15% to Claudio Genu. For completing these payments, they used contracts for supplying consulting services, signed by Paulo Roberto Costa.[105] These contracts were formalized through Camargo Correa and Engevix. Gerson Almeida managed the supplying contract with Engevix and Costa Global, and Eduardo Leite, Commercial Vice-President of Camargo Correa, mediated a consultancy contract[106]. In the case of Camargo Correa, the contract price was three million *reais*, paid in monthly fees of R$ 100 thousand. Engevix's contract reached R$ 730 thousand, with a monthly payment of R$ 30 thousand, which were carried out by the operator Carlos Habib Chater, or through in-kind deliveries by the emissaries Rafael Angulo Lopez or Adarico Montenegro.[107]

---

104 Ibid. Page 5.
105 Policia Federal Superintendência Regional No Estado Do Paraná, Delegacia Regional de Combate ao Crime Organizado e Delegacia de Repressão a Crimes contra o Sistema Financeiro e Desvio de Verbas Publicas. (2014). *Termo de Colaboração No. 2 Termo de Declarações que presta Alberto Youssef.* Page 2.
106 Ibid.
107 Ibid.

Pedro Jose Barusco Filho

In 1995, during Pedro Jose Barusco Filho's time as Head of Installation Technology, he received illicit financial contributions from the company SBM, represented at the time by Julio Faerman, for two contracts with the company FPSO.[108] Such unlawful payments occurred from 1995 to 2003, in monthly fees that oscillated between USD$ 25 thousand and USD$ 50 thousand. By 2007, Pedro Barusco was appointed as Executive Engineering Manager and signed several contracts with SBM, obtaining a total of USD$ 22 million, that he then transferred to BBA Credit Stanstalt, finally ending up in Banco Safra. From such contract, Renato de Souza Duque requested to SBM's representative a total amount of USD $300 thousand as a "contribution" to the *Partido dos Trabalhadores* (PT).[109]

According to Pedro Jose Barusco Filho's declaration, from 2003 to 2011, 90 contracts for major constructions were signed between Petrobras and other companies in Brazil.[110] Pedro Jose Barusco, Renato Duque, and the PT through Joao Vaccari Neto, received illegal financial contributions as a result of the mentioned agreements.[111] These contracts were linked to the Supplying, Gas, Energy, Exploration, and Production Management inside Petrobras, as well as the Directorate of Services. Regarding the contracts associated with the Supplying Management, the fee was of 2% of the total value of each contract, which was, in turn, divided

---

108 Policia Federal Superintendência Regional No Estado Do Paraná, Delegacia Regional de Combate ao Crime Organizado e Delegacia de Repressão a Crimines contra o Sistema Financeiro e Desvio de Verbas Publicas. (2014). *Termo de Colaboração No. 03 Termo de Declarações que presta Pedro Jose Barusco Filho.* Page 2.
109 Ibid. Page 3.
110 Ibid.
111 Ibid.

as follows: 1% to Paulo Roberto Costa, who distributed it to the *Partido do Movimento Democrático Brasileiro* and the *Partido Progresista*; the remaining 1% was divided 0.5% to the *Partido dos Trabhaladores* through Joao Vaccari, and 0.5% to Renato Duque, Jorge Luiz Zelade, and Pedro Barusco.[112] Regarding the destination of the remaining percentages, 1% of the total value of each contract was delivered to the *Partido dos Trabhaladores* through Joao Vaccari Neto, and another 1% for "the house", in this context, the Head of the Section.[113]

In the case of the Supplying Management, the major contracts awarded under the described scheme were Refinería Abreu e Lima (RNEST), Complexo Petroquímico do Rio de Janeiro (Comperj), Replan, Revap, Reduc, Relan and Repar;[114] in the case of the Gas and Energy Management initially directed by Ildo Sauer, and later by Maria Das Graça Foster, the main signed contracts were with Gasodutos Gastau, Urucu-Manus, Piers de GNL, Gasduc, and Gascac[115]. The principal contracts in the case of the Exploration and Production Management, under the command of Guilherme Estrela were the P51, P52, P53, P55, P56, P57, P58, P61, and P63 platforms[116]. Finally, in the case of the Directorate of Services, under Renato Duque direction, some relevant contracts were at the *Centro de Pesquisa* (Cenpes) and the *Centro de Processamento de Dados*.[117]

In order to carry out the illegal payments of the awarded contracts, transfers were made through the following

---

112 Ibid.
113 Ibid.
114 Ibid. Page 4.
115 Ibid.
116 Ibid.
117 Ibid.

financial operators: (i) Julio Gerin de Almeida Camargo for Mitsui Toyo and Camargo Correa, (ii) Shinko Nakandakari for Galvao Engenharia, Eit, and Contreiras, (iii) Mario Goes for Utc, Mpe, Oas, Mendes Junio, Andrade Gutierrez, Schain, Carioca, and Bueno Engenharia.[118]

It is estimated that the *Partido dos Trabhaladores* (PT) signed indirectly, through their "*apadrinhados*", between 2003 and 2013, 90 contracts and received USD$ 200 million[119] in bribes; whilst Renato Duque and Pedro Jose Barusco received USD$ 50 million each one for the same number of contracts.[120]

GFD, Alberto Youssef, and Petrobras

Alberto Youssef created the company GFD upon his release from prison to safeguard third parties' wealth. Some individuals involved in this case include Jose Janene, with an inversion of USD$ 13 million, and Nelma Penasso Kodoma, with USD$ 900 thousand.[121] In 2008, Carlos Pereira Costa was included, and later Joao Procopio, Mario Lucio, and Enivaldo Cuadrado. Eventually, the company became a petty cash in which bribe related money was safeguarded and triangulated. Within this triangulation, the one conducted by Sanko and MO Consultoria is worth to highlight, because Camargo Correa hired these companies to formalize the illegal transfers to the *Partido Progressista Brasileiro*.[122]

---

118 Ibid. Page 5.
119 Ibid. Page 7.
120 Ibid
121 Policia Federal Superintendência Regional No Estado Do Paraná, Delegacia Regional de Combate ao Crime Organizado e Delegacia de Repressão a Crimines contra o Sistema Financeiro e Desvio de Verbas Publicas. (2014). *Termo de Colaboração No. 04 Termo de Declarações que presta Alberto Youssef.* Page 2.
122 Ibid. Page 3.

Alberto Youssef and Julio Camargo

Julio Camargo represented Mitsui Toyo, which was part of Petrobras' contracts, and Pirelli, a company dedicated to providing equipment to Petrobras.[123] Julio Camargo was also related to Camargo Correa, since it provided consultancy and management services to Camargo Correa's projects, such as the Brazil-Bolivia gas pipeline, or even construction works executed jointly by Camargo Correa and Mitsui Toyo.[124] Furthermore, Julio Camargo was in charge of delivering the payments to Camargo Correa and Alberto Youssef.[125]

The *modus operandi* consisted of formalizing contracts for providing consultancy, intermediation, and management services between (i) Mitsui Toyo, Camargo Correa, and Pirelli, and (ii) Julio Camargo´s companies, such as Treviso, Auguri, and Piemonte.[126] Through these simulated contracts, Julio Camargo generated surpluses that were available in accounts, as well as properties of Treviso, Auguri, and Piemonte.[127] Julio Camargo then transferred these assets through Agora Corretora, located in Sao Paulo, to a foreign account operated by himself; the outflow of resources was achieved with a distribution of tax-free benefits from Treviso, Auguri, and Piemonte.[128]

---

123 Policia Federal Superintendência Regional No Estado Do Paraná, Delegacia Regional de Combate ao Crime Organizado e Delegacia de Repressão a Crimines contra o Sistema Financeiro e Desvio de Verbas Publicas. (2014). *Termo de Colaboração No. 05 Termo de Declarações que presta Alberto Youssef.* Page 2.
124 Ibid.
125 Ibid.
126 Policia Federal Superintendência Regional No Estado Do Paraná, Delegacia Regional de Combate ao Crime Organizado e Delegacia de Repressão a Crimines contra o Sistema Financeiro e Desvio de Verbas Publicas. (2014). *Termo de Colaboração No. 08 Termo de Declarações que presta Alberto Youssef.* Page 2
127 Ibid.
128 Ibid.

After the transferred money was available in the intended destination –accounts in Switzerland, Montevideo, United Stated of America, and Italy–, Julio Camargo invested in stocks[129]. Through this process, Julio Camargo conducted, along with foreign banks, operations of loans backed by the stock portfolio; the monetary resources obtained with such loans were destined to certain accounts indicated by Alberto Youssef. One of these accounts, the Devonshire Global opened in the JP Morgan Bank, United States, was registered under the name of Carlos Pereira da Costa although they belonged to Alberto Youssef.[130] Similar accounts were those Leonardo Mirelles under the companies located in Hong Kong Dgx, Gx, Elite Day, and Rfy, as well as offshore accounts property of Nelma Penasso Kodoma and Carlos Rocha´s clients.[131] Then, the account holders delivered the money in cash to Alberto Youssef in Brazil. This *modus operandi* was replicated between 2005 until 2012, allowing to manage around R$ 27 million.[132]

A second *modus operandi* consisted in overvalued contracts regarding the provision of services with Treviso, Piemonte, and Auguri, all registered under Julio Camargo.[133] The surcharge was transferred as investments by the companies to GFD Inversiones. In these contracts, Eduardo Leite, known as "Leitosot", represented Camargo Correas.[134] To execute the transfers, the companies signed mutual agreement contracts. Subsequently, the money was delivered to Alberto Youssef who, in turn, delivered it to Paulo Roberto Costa, Joào Genu, and the

---

129 Ibid
130 Ibid. Page 3.
131 Ibid.
132 Ibid.
133 Ibid.
134 Ibid. Page 4.

Partido Progressista. Such scheme was used during a presidential campaign, between 2010 and 2011, and the approximate total value manipulated was R$ 13 million.[135]

Petrobras and Samsung

In 2004, Samsung and Petrobras signed a contract with the involvement of Mitsui Toyo.[136] To facilitate the contract, it was requested to Julio Camargo, at that time Mitsui Toyo's representative, to pay a percentage as bribes to the *Partido do Movimento Democrático Brasileiro* (PMDB), particularly to the congressman Eduardo Cunha, to Paulo Roberto Costa, and to Nestor Cunate Cervero, director of the International Area of Petrobras.[137] To deliver the payment, Julio Carmargo, delivered the bribes to Fernando Soares, financial operator of the *Partido do Movimento Democrático Brasileiro* (PMDB) at Petrobras, using a contract stablished between him, Julio Carmargo, and Samsung.[138]

During the rent time, Samsung suspended the commissions that Julio Camargo used to receive by serving as an intermediary, although Samsung keep receiving the values associated to the platform ship rent from Petrobras (usually by transactions abroad).[139] In this sense, Julio Camargo sued Samsung in London in order to receive the commissions for his services.[140] When the payment of these commissions stopped, Julio Camargo also ceased the bribe

---

135 Ibid.
136 Policia Federal Superintendência Regional No Estado Do Paraná, Delegacia Regional de Combate ao Crime Organizado e Delegacia de Repressão a Crimes contra o Sistema Financeiro e Desvio de Verbas Publicas. (2014). *Termo de Colaboração No. 13 Termo de Declarações que presta ALBERTO YOUSSEF.* Page 2
137 Ibid.
138 Ibid.
139 Ibid. Page. 3
140 Ibid.

payments of Fernando Soares. When this occurred, Eduardo Cunha pressured Julio Camargo, through the Deputy's Chamber, to make him continue the bribe payments to Fernando Soares (in behalf of the *Partido do Movimento Democrático Brasileiro* (PMDB). Bowing to the pressure, Julio Camargo itself payed R$ 6 million in cash to Fernando Soares, through Alberto Youssef.[141]

Braskem and Petrobras

Braskem is a company dedicated to purchasing Petrobras' products such as naphtha and propane, among others. In 2006, Alexandrino, Braskem's high official, approached Jose Janene to convince him that Braskem should purchase Petrobras' products, since Petrobras' prices in the internal market were lower[142]. Jose Janene, along with Paulo Roberto Costa, adjusted the prices to match the international market and, in exchange, Braskem was requested to pay an annual fee of US$ 5 million, from which 30% was handed to Paulo Roberto Costa and the rest to the *Partido Progessista*.[143]

Braskem's President, Jose Carlos, confirmed the terms of the unlawful agreement. After that, Alberto Youssef and Alexandrino met yearly, along with Jose Janene, Paulo Roberto Costa, and Joào Genu, to define the terms of every agreement and the bribe payments plan of each year.[144] Those meetings took place since 2006 till the year Paulo Roberto Costa left his position as Supply Director

---

141 Ibid.
142 Policia Federal Superintendência Regional No Estado Do Paraná, Delegacia Regional de Combate ao Crime Organizado e Delegacia de Repressão a Crimines contra o Sistema Financeiro e Desvio de Verbas Publicas. (2014). *Termo de Colaboração No. 16 Termo de Declarações que presta ALBERTO YOUSSEF*. Page 2.
143 Ibid.
144 Ibid.

at Petrobras in 2012. The bribe payments initially were transferred through the offshore accounts of the subsidiary companies of Braskem, following indications of Alberto Yousseff. Some of the accounts used to carry this operation were the ones of Nelma Penasso Kodama, Carlos Alexandre Rocha and Leonardo Meirelles (RFY, DGX, and Elite Day)[145]. After the transactions were carried, Alberto Yousseff had the responsibility of delivering the percentage assigned to Joao Genu, Paulo Roberto Costa and Jose Janene.[146]

Petrobras, Quattor, and Unipar

By 2005, the owner of Unipar contacted Jose Janene to create a new company named Quattor in partnership with Petrobras, emerging as competition to Braskem, to dominate the market at that time[147]. The meeting happened in Sao Paulo, where Alberto Youssef, Jose Janene, Joao Genu, and Frank Abubakir, manager and major shareholder of Unipar, were introduced to Jose Octavio Vianello de Melo, Unipar's financial manager.[148] It was agreed that the illegal commission for this project would reach R\$18 million, to be paid to Janene.[149]

Then, Mario Negromonte intervened, and the commission was finally paid to him.[150] Janene insisted on Negromonte to pay to the *Partido Progressista*, as he had accepted the offer.

However, Jose Janene was unsatisfied with the process,

---

145 Ibid.
146 Ibid.
147 Policia Federal Superintendência Regional No Estado Do Paraná, Delegacia Regional de Combate ao Crime Organizado e Delegacia de Repressão a Crimines contra o Sistema Financeiro e Desvio de Verbas Publicas. (2014). *Termo de Colaboração No. 30 Termo de Declarações que presta Alberto Youssef.* Page 2.
148 Ibid.
149 Ibid.
150 Ibid.

and decided to charge Quattor directly for the rest of the value; and for that purpose, another meeting between Joao Genu, Frank Abubakir, Jose Janene, Alberto Youssef, and Jose Octavio Vianello de Melo happened in Sao Paulo, where they agreed to pay nearly R$ 9 million through transfers in kind and notes issued by MO Consultoria, among other companies linked to Waldomiro de Olivieira.[151]

As a result of these agreements, Quattor would acquire raw material from Petrobras at a lower price.[152] The real value of the product was manipulated under Paulo Roberto Costa's management, to secure Quattor's interests. In return, Quattor had to pay a commission as a percentage of the input price.[153] These fees ranged between 1 and 5 million reais, Then, Braskem acquired Quattor, and the bribe system linked to the raw material supply remained the same.[154]

Partido Progresista

Since 1994 until 2012, a hegemonic group dominated the *Partido Progresista* (PP) [Progressive Party].[155] This group consisted of Jose Janene, Pedro Henry, Pedro Correa, Flavio Derns, Nelson Meurer, João Pizzolati, Mario Negromonte, Luiz Fernando Sobrinho, and José Otávio, under the

---

151 Ibid.
152 Ibid.
153 Ibid. Page. 3.
154 Policia Federal Superintendência Regional No Estado Do Paraná, Delegacia Regional de Combate ao Crime Organizado e Delegacia de Repressão a Crimines contra o Sistema Financeiro e Desvio de Verbas Publicas. (2014). *Termo de Colaboração No. 31 Termo de Declarações que presta Alberto Youssef.* Page 2.
155 Policia Federal Superintendência Regional No Estado Do Paraná, Delegacia Regional de Combate ao Crime Organizado e Delegacia de Repressão a Crimines contra o Sistema Financeiro e Desvio de Verbas Publicas. (2014). *Termo de Colaboração No. 14 Termo de Declarações que presta Alberto Youssef.* Page 2.

leading role of Jose Janene until his death.[156] Then, Mario Negromonte took on as the leader, however, Janene's death weakened the dominant group within the PP.[157] As a result, the commissions paid to the members dropped significantly, which caused inner disputes and the departure of Mario Negromonte.[158]

With the PP's new board, the payments intended for the party were delivered directly to Arthur De Lira, PP's formal leader, through Henry Hoyer De Carvalho.[159] Despite the change of leadership, the payments executed by Alberto Youssef were delivered to the former party members, through Rafael Ángulo Lopes, Adarico Negromonte, and Carlos Alexandre Rocha ("Ceara"), who delivered the money in cash to members of the Congress.[160] The following was the *modus operandi* to complete the payments:[161] the assets were transported in suitcases in chartered flights or hidden in emissaries' bodies in commercial planes. To communicate with the parliamentarians to define the delivery schedule, the emissaries used exclusive phones that changed periodically to prevent wiretapping. This parallel delivery to the former PP group happened between 2005 and 2012.[162]

---

156 Ibid.
157 Ibid.
158 Ibid
159 Ibid. Page 3.
160 Ibid.
161 Ibid.
162 Ibid. Page 4.

Partido do Movimiento Democratico Brasileiro

Since the administration of the former president Jose Sarney, the *Partido do Movimiento Democratico Brasileiro* (PMDB) had strong representation in the Congress, with a core composed by Renan Calheiros, Romero Juca, Eunicio Oliveira, Valdir Raupp, and Edison Lobao, in charge of monopolizing the appointments in the Federal Government, not only concerning energy companies, but also regulatory agencies and ministries.[163] This influence consisted of placing agents in strategic government positions to satisfy the parties' interests, as well as its members. For instance, this was the case of Silas Rondeau Cavalcante Silva, who was appointed in various state-owned companies engaged with production and transmission of energy.[164] In fact, in 2005 Cavalcante Silva even held the position of Minister of Mines and Energy.

Silas Rondeau took advantage of his position as director of Eletrobras, as well as Minister, to facilitate the allocation and development of projects. According to with Delcidio Do Amaral's testimony, Silas approached the companies and introduced himself as a broker on behalf of the PMDB core, offering businesses with eventual trade-offs in the form of illicit financial benefits for the members of that group, such as the cases of Jirau, Angra, and Belo Monte.[165] However, Silas was never a financial operator in those projects, but only an intermediary between companies and political groups.[166]

---

163 Policia Federal Superintendência Regional No Estado Do Paraná, Delegacia Regional de Combate ao Crime Organizado e Delegacia de Repressão a Crimes contra o Sistema Financeiro e Desvio de Verbas Publicas. (2016). *Termo de Colaboração No. 15 Termo de Declarações que presta Delcido Do Amaral Gomez.* Page 2.
164 Ibid. Page 3.
165 Ibid. Page 2.
166 Ibid.

By 2005, after the "Mensalão" scandal, Ignacio Lula Da Silva's administration and the PT lost popularity, which increased the possibilities of party's officials being removed from key positions. Such was the case of Nestor Cervero, International Director of Petrobras, and Paulo Roberto Costa, Supplying Manager of those company.[167] Both officials were linked to the *Partido do Movimiento Democratico Brasileiro* through Silas Rondeau, Minister of Mines and Energy at that time.[168] This resulted in more flexible bidding processes, in order to allow the participating companies to obtain contracts in exchange for their "donations" to the political party.[169] In 2007, Jorge Zelade was appointed as International Director of Petrobras, at the request of the PMDB, including the President Michel Temer.[170]

---

167 Policia Federal Superintendência Regional No Estado Do Paraná, Delegacia Regional de Combate ao Crime Organizado e Delegacia de Repressão a Crimines contra o Sistema Financeiro e Desvio de Verbas Publicas. (2016). *Termo de Colaboração No. 2 Termo de Declarações que presta Delcido Do Amaral Gomez.* Page 3.
168 Ibid. Page. 4.
169 Ibid.
170 Ibid. Page. 5.

Chapter 6: The "Eletrobras Termonuclear S.A. Eletronuclear" Subnetwork

Andrade Gutierrez: Powerful Contractor, Promoter of Corruption and Money Laundering

The Company Andrade Gutierrez and Othon Luiz as a Key Planner and Executive Agent

The illicit substructure established within the company Eletronuclear operated through contracts of services for constructing the Thermonuclear Plant of Angra 3 by Eletrobras Termonuclear S.A. When bank secrecy was lifted for companies Andrade Gutierrez and Engevix, authorities discovered that they were involved in the payment of undue commissions to the former president of Eletronuclear, Othon Luiz, to obtain also unjustified advantages on Angras 3's contracting processes.[171] In fact, the financial statements of Andrade Gutierrez allowed verifying bribe payments to Othon Luiz. Those bribes were

---

171 The scheme in Eletrobras was uncovered due to the information revealed in the plea agreement of Dalton Avancini, former president of Camargo Correa S. A. Autos no. 5055647—04.2014.404.7000. Available in: http://anexos.radaroficial. com.br/e4a126afaaf7e9a9b79c569d1eff9c98.pdf

declared as consulting payments to CG Impex, Engenharia e Representação Comercial Ltda., and Jnobre Engenharia e Consultoria Ltd.[172]

Bruno Gonçalves Luz and Jorge Luz were the financial operators who deposited R$ 276,444.92 (USD$ 85,208.00, approximately) to the company Aratec Engenharia Consultoria & Representaciones Ltda., controlled by Ana Cristina Toniolo, daughter of Othon Luiz. It was also identified that Octavio Marques and Flavio David, under the orders of the president of Andrade Gutierrez, were responsible for planning and executing contracts with Eletronuclear.[173]

Likewise, an interaction was identified between Carlos Alberto Montenegro Gallo, director at CG Iimpex, Víctor Sérgio Colavitti, manager of the company Link Projetos e Participaçes S.A., and the company Andrade Gutierrez, regarding the contracts with both "Petrobras" and Eletronuclear. Victor Sergio Colavitti admitted that paid bribes through his company to Engevix and Aratec, owned by Ana Cristina Bolognani, Ana Luiza Bolognani and Maria Célia da Silva, daughters and wife of Othon Luiz. Also, under the name of the company Hydropower Enterprise Ltd., Ana Cristina, and Ana Luiza Bolognani opened an account at the Banco Havilland S.A. in Luxembourg, to receive bribes using the services of Bernardo Freiburghaus, one of the money laundering operators in the entire Petrobras illicit scheme.[174]

---

172 Poder Judiciário Justiça Federal Seçao Judiciária do Rio de Janeiro. (2016). Sentença processo n° 0510926-86.2015.4.02.5101 Available: http://www.mpf. mp.br/para-o-cidadao/caso-lava-jato/desmembramentos/rio-de-janeiro/ documentos/sentenca-radioatividade, page 50.
173 Ibid. Page 3.
174 Ibid. Page 97.

According to information analyzed by *Ministério Público Federal & Procuradoria-Geral Da República*, the following contracts were obtained with undue advantages provided by Othon Luiz, in exchange for bribes or commission payments:

• Nco-223/83 Contract dated June 10th, 1983: Eletronuclear and Andrade Gutierrez signed this contract for providing works and services to Angra 3. The project began in June 1984 and was suspended in April 1986. On June 25, 2007, the National Council for Energy Policy ("CNPE") authorized reinitiating the project and the contract NCO-223/83 was renegotiated to include additives 21-L, 21-M, 21-N, 21-O, 21-P, 21-Q, 22, 23, 24, 25, 26, 27-A, extending the period and demanding the fraudulent payment of additional services. The total amount of the addition was R$ 1,809,584,629.00 (USD$ 557,786,366.00, approximately) to the original value of the contract.[175]

• Contract Gac.T/Ct-003/007 dated August 13th, 2007: This contract was originally established to build steam generators of Angra 1, valued on R$ 13,457,950.26 (USD$ 4,148,278.00, approximately). Originally signed by Othon Luiz from "Eletronuclear", Clóvis Renato and Andrade Gutierrez, it was later modified with an additive clause dated February 11th, 2008, signed by Othon Luiz from Eletronuclear, Marcos José M. Teixeira, and Andrade Gutierrez, adding a value of R$ 1,498,772.80 (USD$ 461,981.00, approximately).[176]

• Contract Gac.T/Ct-008/05 dated June 21st, 2006: This contract, with an original value of R$ 15,208,074.65

---

175 Ibid. Page 25.
176 Ibid.

was established to build the third deposit and to expand the second deposit of the Management Disposal Center. The contract was signed by Othon Luiz, representing Eletronuclear, Clóvis Renato, and the contractor company on June 21st, 2006. An initial addition increased the value by R$ 1 million 400 thousand, while a second addition modified the term of execution. Othon Luiz from Eletronuclear, Marcos José M. Teixeira and the contracting company signed both modifications on June 22nd, 2007 and December 19th, 2007, respectively.[177]

According to the collaborator Rogério Nora, Othon Luiz requested bribes in 2006 during a meeting at the Andrade Gutierrez' headquarters in Rio de Janeiro. Nora also argued that even before 2006, Othon Luiz has already negotiated in 2006 with Marcos José M. Teixeira, Regional Director of the contractor company.[178]

Likewise, Rogério Nora reported that he met Othon Luiz through Marcos José M. Teixeira and that the defendant, after assuming the presidency of Eletronuclear, requested also undue payments to Andrade Gutierrez for an amount between 20 and 30 thousand *reais*. Marcos José M. Teixeira controlled those payments. With the contracts of Angra 3, the bribes reached 1% of the contracts' value.[179]

To complete the payment of bribes, operator Clovis Renato transferred approximately R$ 4 million to Othon Luiz. After Rogério Nora and Clovis Renato were discharged in 2013, Flávio Barra and Gustavo Botelho executed those payments.[180]

---

177 Ibid. Page 25.
178 Ibid. Page 29.
179 Ibid.
180 Ibid.

According to Flávio Barra's statement, in 2014 Othon Luiz requested a new payment that Gustavo Botelho made through the fraudulent contracting of the company Deustchebras. This transaction involved the transfer of R$ 300 thousand (USD$ 92,472.00, approximately).[181]

Also, Otávio Marques, former president of Andrade Gutierrez stated that since 2008 he began paying "political contributions" through donations to political campaigns. Marques said that the *Partido dos Trabalhadores* made an agreement to obtain 1% on the values of contracts with the federal government, including the contract with Eletronuclear for the civil works of Angra 3. In his statement, Rogério Nora declared that Otávio Marques focused on establishing political agreements, considering that he was mainly involved in the negotiation with the *Partido dos Trabalhadores* and *Partido do Movimento Democrático Brasileiro*.[182]

The Company Andrade Gutierrez as a Powerful Contractor

Between June 25th, 2007, and August 5th, 2015, the defendant Othon Luiz negotiated at least 24 payments of bribes with the company Andrade Gutierrez, for favoring it during tenders, contracts, agreements for amendments, and additives. Clóvis Renato estimated that he transferred between 3 and 4 million *reais* to Othon Luiz,

---

181 Ibid. Page 30.
182 Ibid. Page 30.

cleared through fraudulent contracts elaborated by Olavinho Pereira.[183] Between June 25th, 2007, and August 5th, 2015, Othon Luiz received around R$ 3,438,500,000.00 (USD $ 1,063,183,092.00, approximately) derived from the concession undue advantages to a privileged contractor.[184]

Andrade Gutierrez as an Orchestrator of Massive Money Laundering

Considering the millionaire value of the bribes, it calls the attention that Othon Luiz did not receive bribes under his real account, nor even in kind. With the purpose of keeping the origin of the bribes untraceable, additional illegal agreements were established to formalize fictitious service contracts with companies of Carlos Gallo, Josué Nobre, Geraldo Arruda, and Victor Colavitti, in order to cover up the illicit operation.[185]

Carlos Gallo, Clóvis Renato, Olavinho Ferreira, with the complicity of Flávio Barra, Gustavo Botelho, Rogério Nora,

---

183 It was recorded that the events occurred on the following occasions:
· At the headquarters of "Andrade Gutierrez" with Othon Luiz on 03/26/2008 and 07/17/2008;
· The combination of the 21-L, 21-M, 21-N, 22, 21-O, 21-P, 23, 21-Q, 24, 25, 26, 27 and 27-A additives to the NCO 223 / 83.
· During the execution of Contract Gac.T/CT-008/05 and the settlement of Additive 1.
· During the execution of Contract Gac.T/CT 003/007 and the settlement of Additive 1.
· In the internal and external phase, pre-qualification tender Gac.T/CN-005/1.
· In the internal phase of tender Competition Gac.T/CN-003/13 (before publication of notice of the tender on 05/13/2013).
· In the external phase of the tender Gac.T/CN-003/13 (as of 05/13/2013).
· During the discussion phase of discounts with the consortia UNA 3 and Angra 3 (after the presentation of the offers until the signing of the contracts Gac.T/CT-4500167239 and Gac.T/CT-450016724 on 09/19/2014).
· In the execution phase of contracts Gac.T/CT-4500167239 and Gac.T/CT-450016724 (as of 09/19/2014).
184 Ibid. Page 44.
185 Ibid. Page. 48

Otávio Marques, and Othon Luiz, participated in money laundering operations concealing and disguising the origin, nature, location, disposition, movements and ownership of a total amount of R$ 2 million 930 thousand (USD$ 904.077, approximately)[186], which happened in 13 money laundering events executed by Andrade Gutierrez through CG Impex Engenharia y Representação Comercial Ltda. To materialize this money laundering operation, the following four contracts were established:

• Contract for technical, economic and financial consultancy services, for the analysis of studies related to urban mobility projects such as the connecting road traffic in the metropolitan region of Rio de Janeiro, with a value of R$ 300 thousand (USD$ 92,567.00, approximately) dated February 2nd, 2009. Carlos Gallo signed on behalf of CG Impex, while Clóvis Renato and Olavinho Ferreira signed as witnesses for Andrade Gutierrez.[187]

• Contract for technical, economic and financial consultancy services to optimize costs in the West, East and Northern regions with a value of R$ 1 million (USD$ 308,425.00, approximately), dated March 1st, 2010. Carlos Gallo signed on behalf of CG Impex while Clóvis Renato and Olavinho Ferreira signed as witnesses for Andrade Gutierrez.[188]

• First amendment to the service provision agreement dated September 1st, 2010, with a value of R$ 1 million 330 thousand (USD$ 410,172.00, approximately). Carlos Gallo

---

186 Ibid. Page 51.
187 Ibid.
188 Ibid.

signed on behalf of CG Impex and Clóvis Renato on behalf of Andrade Gutierrez.[189]

• Contract for technical, economic and financial consultancy services dated August 18th, 2011, to optimize costs in public and/or private enterprises in the Southeast region with a value of R$ 1 million 300 thousand (USD$ 401,099.00, approximately). Carlos Gallo on behalf of CG Impex, and Clóvis Renato and Olavinho Ferreira as recipient and witnesses for Andrade Gutierrez, signed the contract.[190]

To justify these contracts, CG Impex issued fraudulent tax invoices for R$ 2 million 930 thousand (USD$ 904,049.00, approximately). According to Flávio Barra's declaration, all the service contracts were fraudulent. This statement was corroborated in the declaration provided by Rogério Nora, confirming that Clóvis Renato operationalized these payments.[191]

Aratec: Money Laundering System Benefiting Othon Luiz and His Family

CG Impex Laundering Money for Aratec

Besides the contracts signed between the companies Andrade Gutierrez and CG Impex, another five fraudulent contracts were established between CG Impex and Aratec, disguising and concealing the origin, nature, location, disposition, movement and ownership of a gross amount of R$ 2,045,001.53 (USD$ 630,529.00, approximately),

---

189 Ibid.
190 Ibid.
191 Ibid.

through 38 transactions with a net value of R$ 1,919,233.94 (USD$ 592,033.00, approximately).[192]

Clóvis Sobrinho, Olavinho Ferreira, Flávio Barra, Gustavo Botelho, Rogério Nora, and Otávio Marques, entrusted Carlos Gallo the task of transferring bribes to Aratec, controlled by Othon Luiz and his family. Specifically, the following five contracts were established with Aratec:

• Technical consulting services contract dated October 31st, 2008, between CG Impex and Aratec for analysis of the Padre Adelino complex at Av. Salim Farah Maluf, SP, with a value of R$ 168 thousand (USD$ 51,841.00, approximately). The contract was signed by Carlos Gallo on behalf of CG Impex, and for Ana Cristina, Othos' daughter, on behalf of Aratec.[193]

• Consulting services contract dated January 15th, 2009, for the electromechanical assembly carried out for obtaining fuels, between CG Impex and Aratec, with a value of R$ 82 thousand (USD$ 25,295.00, approximately). This contract was signed between CG Impex and Aratec.[194]

• Technical consulting services contract dated September 1st, 2009, between CG Impex and Aratec for studying the mechanical functionality of the Padre Adelino complex at Av. Salim Farah Maluf, SP, part 2, with a value of R$ 400 thousand (USD$ 123,373.00, approximately). This contract was also signed between CG Impex and Aratec.[195]

• Consulting services contract dated January 5th, 2010, on the electromechanical assembly at the plants

---

192 Ibid. Page 56.
193 Ibid.
194 Ibid.
195 Ibid.

obtaining fuels, oil and gas R&D, between CG Impex and Aratec, with a value of R$ 250 thousand (USD$ 77,101.00, approximately).[196]

• Provision of services contract dated July 1st, 2010, to analyze the proposal for the pre-salt regulatory framework, valued on R$ 100 thousand (USD$ 30,844.00, approximately).[197]

According to Carlos Gallo, these contracts were fictitious and fraudulent, since CG Impex did not provide any service to Aratec. Ana Cristina admitted that Aratec did not render services to CG Impex and that Othon Luiz and Carlos Gallo decided the reception of the amounts paid to the company.

Jnobre Engenharia Laundering Money for Aratec

Josué Nobre, Clóvis Renato, Olavinho Ferreira, Flávio Barra and Gustavo Botelho, under the guidance and consent of Othon Luiz and Otávio Marques, concealed and disguised the origin, nature, location, arrangement, movement and ownership of R$ 1 million 400 thousand (USD$ 431,891.00, approximately) through five transactions under fictitious contracts established between Andrade Gutierrez and Jnobre Engenharia. Each fraudulent contract was an instrument for money laundering.[198]

Josué Nobre issued fiscal notes in favor of Andrade Gutierrez, with a total value of R$ 1 million 400 thousand. Nobre also acknowledged the existence of a fictitious

---

196 Ibid.
197 Ibid. Page 57.
198 Ibid. Page 59.

contract with the same value of R$ 1 million 400 thousand signed under the guidance of Carlos Gallo.[199]

Once the payments from Andrade Gutierrez were credited to the Jnobre's bank accounts, the defendants Ana Cristina and Josué Nobre, with the participation of Carlos Gallo, simulated contracts of services between Jnobre and Aratec, as well as fraudulent invoices to conceal and disguise the origin, nature, location, disposition, movement and ownership of the gross amount of R$ 927,500.00 (USDS 286,122.00, approximately) to Aratec.[200]

Deutschebras Laundering Money for Aratec

Flávio Barra, Gustavo Botelhol, Geraldo Arruda and Otávio Marques, supervised by Othon Luiz, concealed and disguised the origin, nature, location, disposition, movement, and ownership of R$ 330 thousand (USD$ 101,801.00, approximately), through a single transaction based on a fictitious contract between Andrade Gutierrez and Deutschebras, managed by Geraldo Arruda.[201]

Also, Flávio Barra and Gustavo Botelho signed a fictitious contract between Andrade Gutierrez and Deutschebras on August 15th, 2014, with a value of R $330 thousand, aimed to provide services for a project to design security systems for floors 14 to 20 of the Oscar Niemeyer Tower.[202]

Regarding the same company, Geraldo Arruda, Flávio Barra, Ana Cristina, Gustavo Botelho, Otávio Marques and Othon Luiz simulated a service contract between

---

199 Ibid. Page 60.
200 Ibid.
201 Ibid. Page 64.
202 Ibid.

Deutschebras and Aratec to conceal and disguise the origin, nature, location, disposition, movement and ownership of the amount of R $252,300.00 (USD$ 77,827.00, approximately) on December 12th, 2014.[203]

Active Corruption by CG Engevix S.A.

Co-opting the Contracting Process of Eletronuclear

According to the indictment, the representatives of Engevix, José Antunes and Cristiano Kok, offered and promised 29 times improper bribe payments to the defendant Othon Luiz to omit or delay an act of office due to the approach that the Eletronuclear President adopted during various tenders and contracts,[204] as follows:

• Contract CT-141 between Engevix S.A. and Eletronuclear (Bidding process GAC.T - 009/05 - addendum 16): Signed on February 17th, 1982, for executing engineering and consultancy for the civil construction works at the Almirante Alvaro Alberto Nuclear Power Plant, Units 2 and 3 (Angra 2 and Angra 3). With the sixteenth addition dated July 29th, 2005, the object of the contract was restrained to the withdrawal of Angra 2. After resuming the construction of the Angra 3 Plant (Resolution No. 3 of CNPE on June 25th, 2007)

---

203 Ibid. Page 66.

204 As a result, Othon Luiz suspended practicing official acts, violating the following official duties: 1. Preparing the edicts in tenders: Gac.T/CN 003/2010, Gac.T/CN 005/2010, GAT.CN/006/2010, Gac.T/CV 027/2-11, Gac.T.CV 041/2011 and Gac.T/CN-012/2012 of Eletronuclear; 2. Fixing the additive 19 and the execution of contract CT-141, 3. Executing contract Gac.T/CT-033/10, Gac.T/CT-4500136548, GAC.T/AS-4500145718, Gac.T/CT 4500146846, Gac.T/AS 4500149995; Gac.T/ CT 4500160692 all signed between Engevix and Eletronuclear; and, Gac.T/CT-4500151462 signed between AF Consult and Eletronuclear.

there were negotiations for amendments to the original contract (Additive 19) between Engevix and Eletronuclear. The Additive 19, dated June 4th, 2012, was signed by Othon Luiz, Sergio Capellão, Ronaldo Ferreira, revising the twenty-first clause of the contract CT-141. The total value of the original contract, R$ 7 million 700 thousand (USD$ 2,375,229.00, approximately), increased to R$ 12 million 347 thousand (USD$ 3,808,695.00, approximately).[205]

• Call for tender Gac.T/CN-005/2010 (Procedure Gac.T-034/09) and Contract Gac.T/Ct- 033/10: The call for tender Gac.T/CN-005/2010 was published on May 28th, 2010, for contracting specialized technical services of civilengineering (package 1: calculations of structure of Angra 3), opting for the modality of technical tender and pricing. The companies Engevix, Gempro and Intertechne took part in the tender although the only qualified company was Intertechne with a proposal of R$ 13,492,938.88 (USD$ 4,162,495.00, approximately), versus the Engevix proposal of R$ 14,274,091.09 (USD$ 4,403,273.00, approximately). Engevix ranked first in the contest based on the evaluation of the proposal adopting a Technical Index, signing the contract GAC.T/CT-033/10 for providing specialized technical engineering services (Civil Package 1 - Structural calculations of Units 3), with an original value of R$ 13,979,888.05 (USD$ 4,312,496.00, approximately). Othon Luiz from Eletronuclear and Sergio Luiz F. Capellão from Engevix signed this contract. On February 8th, 2012, the first additive amendment was signed to increase the contract value to R $2,977,258.35 (USD$ 918,330.00, approximately).[206]

---

205 Ibid. Page 75.
206 Ibid. Page 76.

• Call Notice Gac.T/CN-003/2010 (Procedure Gac. T004/10) and Contract Gac.T/CT- 4500136548: The purpose of the call for tenders Gac.T/CN-003/2010, published

on May 28th, 2010, was to provide specialized technical services for the Pipe Project of the External Area and Tubovia Interconnection of Unit 3 with Unit 2 of Angra 3, also in the modality of technical tender and pricing. Engevix, Cappe, Chemtec, Genpro, and Marte attended the call, of which only Marte with a proposal of R$ 2,720,600.00 (USD$ 839,204.00, approximately), and Engevix, with a proposal of R$ 2,336,983.27 (USD$ 720,885.00, approximately), were authorized to participate. On March 30th, 2011, Engevix won the tender Gac.T/CT-4500136548 with an original value of R$ 2,288,791.70 (USD$ 705,974.00, approximately). On February 2nd, 2012, an amendment (form 1) was introduced to the contract, altering annexes without the modification of the contractual value. The second and third additives dated November 1st, 2012, and June 5th, 2014, respectively, modified the period of execution of the contracted services.[207]

• Call Gac.T/CV-027/2011 (Procedure Gac.T-029/11) and Contract Gac.T/As- 4500145718: On November 17th, 2011, Eletronuclear published the call to tender Gac.T/CV-027/2011, for the provision of engineering services related to the preparation of executive projects for the Support building, Extension of the Gateway and Floating Dock at the Beach of the Frade at Angra dos Reis Municipality. The companies Engevix, Leme, and Nitrio took part in the tender. Engevix won the tender and signed with Eletronuclear the contract Gac.T/AS-4500145718 with an original value of R$ 118,800.00 (USD$ 36,647.00, approximately). The first Additive was signed on March 5th, 2012, to extend the period

---

207 Ibid.

of execution of services for 120 calendar days.[208] Call Gac.T/CN-006/2010 (Process Gac.T-033/09) and Contract Gac.T.

CT-4500146846: The call for tender Gac.T/CN-006/2010 was published on May 28th, 2010, with the purpose of providing specialized engineering technical services to the Electromechanical Package 2 associated to the Secondary Unit 3 of Angra 3. The following companies participated in the tender: Intertechne with a proposal of R$ 109,106,400.73 (USD$ 33,657,047.00, approximately), Marte with a proposal of R$ 119,600,000.00 (USD$ 36,893,881.00, approximately), Leme that presented a proposal of R$ 122,422,326.00 (USD$ 37,764,504.00, approximately) and Engevix with R $ 109,078 .994.54 (USD$ 33,647,361.00, approximately).[209] After evaluating the proposals, based on the Technical Index, Engevix qualified as first place in the contest, signing on December 21st, 2011, the contract Gac.T/CT-4500146846 with a value of R $109,098,115.07 (USD$ 33,647,361.00, approximately). On November 11th, 2013, the Additive 1 was signed, modifying the contractual clauses related to the conditions of payment and invoicing. Then, on March 31st, 2014, the Additive 2 modified contractual clauses and increased the value of the contract to R$ 14,746,428.48 (USD$ 4,549,128.00, approximately), increasing its total value R$ 123,844,543.55 (USD$ 38,204,828.00, approximately). On December 8th, 2014, the Additive 3 was signed, which included a specific waiver clause and altered the contractual annex.[210]

• Call Gac.T/CV-041/11 (Process 053/11) and contract Gac.T/As-4500149995: On March 6th, 2012, the call for tender Gac.T/CV-041/2011 through invitation letter

---

208 Ibid.
209 Ibid. Page 77.
210 Ibid.

was published for contracting engineering services for the "Elaboration of the Executive and Legal Projects of the Construction of the Gateway and Floating Attractive in the Red Beach, Municipality of Angra dos Reis – RJ". The companies Engevix, Leme, Engeservice and Nitrio attended the tender. Leme did not submit a proposal.

Engevix proposed R$ 106,800.00, Nitrio R $110,300.00 and Engeservice R$ 259 thousand. Engevix was the winner and signed the contract Gac.T/AS–4500149995 on March 6th, 2012, with an original value of R$ 103 thousand (USD$ 31,773.00, approximately) on December 2011.[211]

• Call Notice Gac.T/CN–012/2012 (Process Gac.T–006/12) and contract Gac.T/As–4500160692: On June 26th, 2012, the call for tender Gac.T/CN–012/2012 was published, to hire Specialized Technical Services for Engineering Civil Package 2 - Construction Projects of Units 3 of Angra 3. The companies authorized were Genpro with a proposal of R$ 9,210,717.29; Intertechne with a proposal of R$ 10,799,009.20; Sei, with a proposal of R$ 11,113,495.81; Epc with a proposal of R$ 11,578,225.18; Leme with a proposal of R$ 11,731,855.86; and Engevix with a proposal of R$ 11,827,233.72.[212]

• Call notice Gac.T/CO.I–004/2010 and contract Gac.T/CT– 4500151462: The invitation to tender Gac.T/CO.I–004/2010 was published on May 28th, 2010, calling for an international competition to hire specialized technical engineering services for the electromechanical package 1 associated with the primary Unit 3 of Angra 3. The company AF Consult Ltd. Finland won, acquiring the commitment

---

211 Ibid. Page 78.
212 Ibid.

that 100% of the services contracted should be made in Brazil. By contractual requirement, AF Consult Ltd. Finland subcontracted the companies AF Consult Ltda. Brazil and Engevix. The Nuclear Plant Area contract was signed on May 24th, 2012, with a value of R$ 162,214,551.43 (USD$ 50,037,761.00, approximately), and it was agreed that 80% of the payments would be made in Brazil and the remaining 20% abroad (contract Electromechanical 1). On December 8th, 2014, the 1st amendment additive was agreed, increasing 4.07% of the original value of the contract.[213]

The proposals submitted by Genpro and Leme Engenharia, despite being the lowest priced, were declassified adducing they presented unitary prices above 7% of the budgeted values for some individual items. Based on the evaluation

of the proposal, Engevix ranked first with an adjusted proposal of R $11,305,663.41 (USD$ 3,487,474.00). Thus, on March 5, 2012, Engevix signed the contract Gac.T/AS-4500160692 with an original value of R$ 11,305,663.41 (USD$ 3,487,474.00).[214]

Link as an Intermediary of Engevix

Jose Antunes and Cristiano Kok, executives of Engevix, offered and promised undue advantages to Othon Luiz to execute, omit and delay decisions related to his functions between June 25th, 2007, and May 08th, 2015. "Engevix" simulated contracts with the company Link Projetos on May 30th, 2010, as a strategy to launder money related to bribes paid to Othon Luiz.[215]

213 Ibid. Page 79.
214 Ibid. Page 78.
215 Ibid. Page 87.

As a result, José Antunes, Cristiano Kok, and Victor Colavitti, with the compliance of Othon Luiz, concealed and disguised the origin, nature, location, disposition,

movement and ownership of a gross amount of R$1,529,166.00 (USD$ 471,715.00, approximately) in 44 transactions. These transactions were sustained on four fictitious contracts established between Engevix and Link Projetos. To conceal the origin of the money, the following contracts were signed.[216]

• Contract 4000/00-M0-PJ-1050/10 dated May 30th, 2010, for R$ 500 thousand (USD$ 154,233.00, approximately), fragmented in 16 payments of R$ 31,250.00 (USD$ 9,639.00, approximately) each one.

• Contract AX0001-00-X0-PJ-0196-12 dated May 24th, 2012, for R$ 250 thousand (USD$ 77,117.00) divided into

eight payments of R$ 31,250.00 (USD$ 9.639.00, approximately) each one.

• Contract AX0001/00-X0-PJ-0264-13 dated January 15th, 2013, for R$ 250 thousand (USD$ 77,117.00, approximately), the first portion with a value of R$ 31,250.00 (USD$ 9,639.00, approximately) and the others for R$ 14,583.00 each one.

• Contract AC001/00-C0-PJ/0058-14 dated January 21st, 2014, with a value of R$ 450 thousand (USD$ 138,818.00, approximately) fragmented into 12 shares of R$ 37,500.00 (USD$ 11,568.00, approximately) each one.

Once the payments from Engevix were credited to Link's accounts, defendants Ana Cristina and Victor Colavitti

---

216 Ibid.

simulated contracts for the provision of services between Link and Aratec to justify the transfer of R$ 1 million (USD$ 308.498.00, approximately) through 35 transfers to Aratec.[217]

José Antunes, Cristiano Kok, and Ana Cristina, also concealed and disguised the nature and movement of R$ 30 thousand (USD$ 9,254.00, approximately) through a transaction between Engevix and Aratec to provide consulting services to the company of Othon Luiz. To conceal and disguise the nature and movement of such amount, Ana Cristina issued on December 11th, 2014, the invoice 620/2015 with a value of R$ 30 thousand related with consulting services presumably provided by Aratec in favor of Engevix. This amount was transferred to Othon Luiz on January 8th, 2015.[218]

Finally, Othon Luiz, with the compliance of his daughter Ana Cristina, kept the amount of R$ 185,797.01 (USD$ 57,318.00, approximately) in the accounts LU36 3184 0287 8000 OUSD and 00402878_0 at the *Banque Havilland* in Luxembourg, on behalf of the offshore company Hydro Power Enterprise Ltd. without declaring the existence of these values to the Brazilian Central Bank. These values resulted directly or indirectly from illicit activities and were held in the offshore accounts between October 10th, 2014, and August 17th, 2015. Ana Cristina opened the account in August 2014, on behalf of a company located in Hong Kong, which was owned by Well Channel Ltd., also registered in Hong Kong, whose belongs to Ana Cristina and her sister Ana Luíza Barbosa de Silva Bolognani.[219]

---

217 Ibid. Page 89.
218 Ibid. Page 90.
219 Ibid. Page 91.

Angra's Electromechanical Assembly Services: Co-opting Seven Colluded Contractors

Internal tender phase

The Brazilian Public Ministry revealed that the negotiation between the representatives of the contracting companies and Othon Luiz happened even before the publication of the Edict GAG.T/CN-005/11, on August 11th, 2011.

Therefore, the edict may have been specially designed to fulfill the interests of companies involved through restrictive clauses to exclude other potential bidders in the qualification phase.[220]

During the plea, based on the special agreement between the Public Ministry and Dalton Avancini, it was stated that Luis Carlos Martins, former Director of Energy at Eletronuclear, and the representatives of Camargo Correa, UTC, Odebrecht, Andrade Gutierrez, Queiroz Galvão, Techint and Ebe modified the edict to benefit these seven contractors. This information was confirmed during the hearing held on December 14th, 2015, in which the adjustments of clauses to restrict competitiveness were confirmed, limiting the number of companies that could qualify and therefore favoring few contractors with "long experience in this type of work".[221]

Dalton Avancini also stated that there was a joint decision between the contracting companies and Eletronuclear to maintain the requirements of the edict and, therefore, to continue benefiting those contractors involved.

---

220 Ibid. Page 35.
221 Ibid.

External Tendering Phase

The evidence suggests that Othon Luiz was not only aware of the collusion between the companies, but that he was also directly involved in setting up the cartel's strategy, as shown with the e-mails exchanged between the directors of the contractors on November 8th and 12th, 2013.[222]

In fact, the collaborator Ricardo Pessoa confirmed that Angramon Consortium was contacted by e-mail for a meeting at UTC headquarters, on June 1st, 2014, to discuss how to pay undue commissions to the Ministry of Mines and Energy and the TCU (Court of Accounts). The collaborator Dalton Avancini confirmed his participation in that meeting, in which it was also discussed the scheme of cartelization and the payments of bribes for the contracts with Eletronuclear. Flávio Barra, from Andrade Gutierrez, Ricardo Ourich from Technit, Ricardo Pessoa from UTC, Fabio Gandolfo from Odebrecht, Renato from EBE, and Petrônio from Queiroz Galvo attended the meeting.[223]

Other businesspersons such as Gustavo Botelho from Andrade Gutierrez and Luiz Carlos from Camargo Correa, testified that in 2009 they participated in a meeting with the group of companies interested in forming a consortium to participate in the tender. They also stated that there were previous meetings with Othon Luiz and other representatives of Eletronuclear to discuss bribes in exchange for undue advantages in tenders.[224]

---

222 Ibid. Page 38.
223 Ibid.
224 Ibid. Page 39.

Chapter 7. The "Sergio Cabral" and "Marco Antonio di Luca" Sub-networks

Sergio Cabral: Corruption in the State of Rio

According to the investigation carried out during the operations "Calicute" and "Eficiencia", an illicit structure articulated by the former governor of Rio de Janeiro, Sergio Cabral, was revealed, involving criminal activities of corruption and money laundering. According to the sources, this sub-network diverted more than R$ 100 billion (USD 30.848.216, approximately) from the public budget, through transfers of assets abroad. Since Sergio Cabral took office as Chief Executive of the State of Rio de Janeiro on January 1st, 2007, he instituted a bribe rate of 5% that applied to every administrative contract with the State.[225]

Through a plea agreement signed with Renato Hasson Chebar and Marcelo Hasson Chebar, it was revealed that Sergio Cabral used Renato Chebar, a financial market operator, to hide in foreign bank accounts the flows of money resulting of the bribes he received in Brazil. One of

---

225 Ministério Público Federal & Procuraduria da República no Estado do Rio de Janeiro. (2017). *Processo de autos n° 0504048-77.2017.4.02.5101; Autos n° 0503012-97.2017.4.02.5101.*

the corruption cases involving Sergio Cabral includes the maintenance of the *Maracaná* Stadium, the PAC-Favels and the construction of The Metropolitan Arch of the State of Rio de Janeiro.[226]

With the purpose of illustrating this illicit structure, it is necessary to identify 4 cores: (i) the political core established by the leader of the criminal organization, Sergio Cabral, (ii) the economic core formed by the executives of the contracted corporations executing projects in the State, (iii) the administrative core consisting of State's managers, and (d) the financial and operational core, which consists of individuals in charge of receiving the bribes and laundering the money.[227]

The complaint lodged by the Public Prosecutor's Office within the framework of the Calicute Operation, identifies two illicit events: active and passive corruption and subsequent asset laundering around contracts concluded between the Rio de Janeiro government and Andrade Gutierrez, Delta, Carioca Engenharia, Oas, Queiroz Galvao, Camargo Correa, Camter, Eit and Odebrecht, as well as the companies used within the money laundering scheme.[228]

The identified facts can be summarized as follows: the executive heads of Delta, Andrade Gutierrez, Carioca Engenharia, Odebrecht, Oas, Queiroz Galvao, Camargo Correa, Camter and Eit created a cartelized group that acted to remove competition in tenders for public works in the State of Rio de Janeiro. In order to win such bidding processes, this group stablished illegal agreements with public officials

---

226 Ibid.
227 Ibid.
228 Ibid.

to avoid deceptive practices in tenders. In this particular case, the group of companies promised to pay to the former Governor, Sergio Cabral, the former Secretary of State, Wilson Carlos, and the Under-Secretary of Public Works, Hudson Braga, a bribe of 5% of the contract's total value for future works. As a result of these preliminary deals, it was possible to eliminate potential competition through the development of calls for tender in which the requirements were only fulfilled by the cartelized companies.[229]

OAS and Odebrecht: Fraud in Public Tender and Restoration of Maracaná Stadium

Between mid-2009 and august 11th, 2010, Sergio Cabral, Wilson Carlos, Hudson Braga, Louzival Luis Lago Mascarenhas Junior and Marcos Antonio Borghi –representing OAS–, Fernando Cavendish –represening Delta–, and Benedicto Barbosa Junio, Eduardo Soares Martins and Irineu Berardi Miereles –representing Odebrecht–, committed fraud through bidding adjustments for the restoration and modernization of the *Maracaná* Stadium.

According to the investigations, anti-competitive agreements between these constructing companies and the Rio de Janeiro government were stablished in June 2009 to obtain undue advantages during the public tender. For instance, it was agreed the regulatory pricing, as well as conditions and advantages for the companies involved in the constructing works. Moreover, a market segmentation was also agreed, allowing the formation of a consortium,

---

229 Ibid.

and the removal of proposals to create the appearance of legality during the tender procedures. This illicit structure operated over the national territory controlling the works of renovation, modernization and construction of stadiums for the World Cup 2014.

Before the call for tender, the Governor Cabral assigned the renovation of the *Maracaná* Stadium to Odebrecht and Delta. In order to take part, Andrade Gutierrez negotiated with Odebrecht a percentage in other works in which the company participated. After that, Odebrecht and Andrade Gutierrez agreed to pay 5% of the value of the contract, each one, to Sergio Cabral as a retribution for winning the tender.

In the context of the dynamic developed by this illicit structure to provide legitimacy to the bidding contest, the company OAS participated with a considerably more expensive proposal than the rest of the consortium, so it seemed that the winning consortium was elected due to the advantageous price and technical issues. To establish this agreement, the representatives of the companies OAS and Odebrecht met in several occasions: December 8th, 2009; December 15th, 2009; December 17th, 2009; January 4th, 2010; January 6th, 2010; February 1st, 2009, and February 11th, 2010. Once OAS and Odebrecht agreed on the conditions, the companies presented their proposals in the contest to give an image of formal competitiveness.

According to an analysis presented by the Court of Auditors of the Union, the existence of overprices in the winner proposal was required to obtain greater public resources through the *Banco Nacional do Desenvolvimento* (BNDES). In addition to this initial surcharge, 16 contractual additions were presented, which increased the initial price of the work stated on R\$ 720 million (USD\$ 222.099.237, approximately) to the final price of R\$ 1,201,740,672.43 million (USD\$ 370.702.342, approximately), of which R\$ 1,198,220,000 (USD 369.621.122 approximately) were paid. It should be noted that such a high a price increase, was only plausible with the collaboration of Sergio Cabral and his illicit organization that controlled every work and verified the overall execution of the project.

Fraud in Public Tenders for Pac-Favelas Works

Between May 10th, 2007, and February, 2008, Sergio Cabral, Wilson Carlos, Hudson Braga and Caro Moreno Junio, former president of the *Empresa de Obras Publicas* (EMOP) in collaboration with Juarez Miranda Junior, representative of Camter; Benedicto Junior, Marcos Vidigal do Amara and Karine Karaoglan Khoury Ribeiro, representatives of Odebrecht; Marcelo Duarte Ribeiro, representative of OAS; Mauricio Rizo and Gustavo Souza, representative of Queiroz Galvao; Paulo Meriade Duarte, representative of Delta; Paulo Cesar Almeida Cabral, representative of EIT; Jose Gilmar Francisco de Santana, representative of Camargo Correa; Ricardo Pernambuco, shareholder of Carioca Engenharia; as well as representatives of Andrade Gutierrez, successfully controlled the bidding contracts of the project called PAC-Favelas, through artificial fixing of prices and quantities sold and produced, illegal agreements with public officials and modifications in the calls for tenders.

In order to illustrate chronologically the actions of the illicit scheme, the events will be explained in 3 phases: (i) before the bidding, (ii) during the bidding, and (iii) during the execution of the construction contract.

Phase I: Before the Bidding

The first phase of the illegal agreements between companies and public officials happened between May 7th and 10th, 2007, in the Guanabara Palace. At that meeting, Wilson Carlos revealed to the representatives of the companies the urbanization project of the favelas *Rocinha*, *Manguitos*, and *Alemao*. Carlos indicated that the works would be tendered in 3 different lots and that the public tender should be led by the companies Queiroz Galvao, Andrade Gutierrez and Odebrecht, due to their contributions to the political campaign of Sergio Cabral in 2006.

It was also agreed on a meeting with Icaro Moreno Junior, by that time president of *Empresa de Obras Publicas* (EMOP), which was the entity in charge of supervising the execution of the works. On May 11th, 2007, a meeting was held between the representatives of the companies and the president of the EMOP to establish that the companies participating in the public tenders would be: Andrade Gutierrez, Carioca, OAS, Odebrecht and Queiroz Galvao. Also, under the instructions of Sergio Cabral, one of the consortiums would have to include the company Delta. In this sense, the following consortiums were established: (i) Novos Tempos Consortium, which was led by Queiroz Galvao, Caenge, and Carioca, choose to win the *Rocinha* lot; (ii) Consorcio Manguinhos, led by Andrade Gutierrez, Camargo Correa, Camter and Eit, destined to win the *Complexo Manguinhos* lot; (iii) Consorcio Rio Melhor, led by Odebrecht, Delta and OAS, destined to conquer the *Complexo do Alemao* lot.

Icaro Moreno Junior asked the companies to approach the architect Hamilton Paes Case and recruit him for the preparation of the project proposal. Since May 14th, 2007, several meetings were held with Hamilton Paes Case to identify the characteristics that should include the technical requirements to obtain federal resources. In May 2007, another meeting was held between the group and Hamilton Paes, where it was agreed to work in the Carioca company's offices, specifically establishing the bidding requirements to eliminate the companies that weren't part of the illicit group. It is important to highlight that it was during the first meeting with Wilson Carlos, when it was established that each consortium had to pay 5% of the contract to Sergio Cabral, to secure their victory during the public tender.

As happened in the *Maracaná* Stadium works, companies established absurd bidding requirements related to technical expertise to eliminate competition; however, market requirements were also established. As an example of these requirements, Odebrecht established that the company winning the bidding of the Complex of Alemao was required to have experience in implementing cable cars. To this end, Odebrecht previously signed an exclusive commercial agreement with the French company Pomagalasky, which installed cable cars in Medellin, Colombia, and which was virtually the only company available to meet the requirements of the tender.

Phase II: During the Public Tender

The call for tender was open to the public until November 26th, 2007; however, it was entangled on December 26th, 2007, when the companies of the illicit scheme decided to change the procedure of participating in the contest. Between November 26th and December 12th, 2007, three meetings happened between representatives of companies and public officials to modify some clauses that were established in the tender.

Between January and February 2008, the consortia agreed to participate in the tender phase. On February 1st, 2008, results of the bidding process were announced with the list of the consortiums that would participate in the illicit scheme.

Phase 3: During the Execution of the Contract

As it happened with the works for the *Maracaná* Stadium, the initial proposals included overpriced items and during the execution additions to the original contract were introduced. As a result, prices increased by 24%, R$ 166,105,466.62 (USD 51.238.937, approximately) for the total of the 3 lots.

Marco Antonio de Luca

During the judicial interrogation carried out in May, 2017, under the criminal action of the auto number 0509503-57.2016.4.02.5101, Luiz Carlos Bezerra admitted that the annotations on his seized notebooks registered the parallel accounting of bribes, and that the alias "Crazy" or "De Louco" referred to Marco Antonio de Luca, linked to the company Frescato. Marco Antonio de Luca was also a partner and administrator of Masan Servicios Especializados Ltda.

As a result of the seized notebooks, parallel accounting controls of bribes by Carlos Bezerra revealed that during the collection of undue advantages the criminal organization led by Sergio Cabral collected between October, 2013, and November, 2016, at least R$ 37,642,500.00 (USD11.612.605, approximately). Marco Antonio de Luca delivered the total of R$ 12,595,700.00 (USD 3.885.985, approximately) to the illicit organization led by Sergio Cabral, through Luiz Carlos Bezerra.

Additionally, the financial intelligence report number 15893 lists 27 suspicious financial in-kind transactions executed by Marco Antonio de Luca. The report notes that between 2014 and 2015, Marco Antonio de Luca carried out in-kind operations by R$ 3,491,499.00 (USD1.077.118, approximately), mainly through the company Masan Comercial Distribuidora. During that period, Marco Antonio de Luca was one of the partners and manager of the company, with 82.7% of shareholding.

Before 2011, Masan Servicios Especializados Ltda. signed the contract No. 6466 with the State Health Fund, State of Rio de Janeiro, for R$ 609,585.00 (USD 188.059, approximately) in 2007. Then, in 2008 Masan signed the contract No. 11024 with the Civil Police of the State of Rio de Janeiro, with a value of R$ 2,398,122.00 (USD 739.857, approximately). In 2010, the number of contracts increased, as well as the amendments, tripling the value originally contracted in 2009.

According to the reports of the Rio de Janeiro State Transparency website, Masan Servicios Especializados Ltda. received a total of R$ 2,111,816,957.80 (USD

651.499.135, approximately) for contracts signed with the State of Rio de Janeiro between 2011 and 2017[230] as follows:

• In 2011: 9 contracts with a value of R$ 25.573.668,80 (USD$ 7.889.552, approximately).

• In 2012: 12 contracts totaling R$ 68.970.557,93 (USD$ 21.277.620, approximately).

• In 2013: 21 contracts totaling R$ 219.282.364,46 (USD$ 67.649.536, approximately).

• In 2014: 24 contracts totaling R$ 520.049.054,73 (USD$ 160.437.332, approximately).

• In 2015: 26 contracts totaling R$ 678.031.261,93 (USD$ 209.175.511, approximately).

• In 2016: 23 contracts totaling R$ 1.802.269.044,16 (USD$ 555.967.041, approximately).

• In 2017: 19 contracts totaling R$ 2.111.816.957,80 (USD$ 651.456.912, approximately).

However, the contractual relationship between the companies directed by Marco Antonio de Luca with the State of Rio de Janeiro did not stop there. The company Comercial Milano Brasil Ltda., that belonged to the same family group, likewise signed dozens of contracts with the State of Rio de Janeiro between 2011 and 2017, increasing every year the values received from the public:[231]

---

230 Ministério Público Federal & Procuraduria da Repúliba no Estado do Rio de Janeiro. (2016) *Processo de autos n° 0509503-57.2016.4.02.5101.* Source: http://politica.estadao.com.br/blogs/fausto-macedo/wp-content/uploads/sites/41/2017/11/75959255-1233-1-pp.pdf.
231 Ibid.

• In 2007: 53 contracts with a total value of R$ 48.905.531,00 (USD$ 15.087.429, approximately).

• In 2008: 31 contracts totaling R$ 33.237.798,00 (USD$ 10.253.910, approximately).

• In 2009: 42 contracts totaling R$ 40.337.022,00 (USD$ 12.444.137, approximately).

• In 2010: 51 contracts totaling R$ 70.483.262,00 (USD$ 21.744.376, approximately).

• In 2011: 61 contracts totaling of R$ 87.471.123,92 (USD$ 26.986.293, approximately).

• In 2012: 71 contracts totaling R$ 117.293.252,17 (USD$ 36.186.915, approximately).

• In 2013: 81 contracts totaling R$ 165.478.696,27 (USD$ 51.052.925, approximately).

• In 2014: 92 contracts totaling R$ 223.513.727,22 (USD$ 68.953.437, approximately).

• In 2015: 101 contracts totaling R$ 252.012.232,84 (USD$ 77.742.992, approximately).

• In 2016: 41 contracts totaling R$ 300.228.386,67 (USD$ 92.617.143, approximately).

• In 2017, 31 contracts. Value R$ 265.968.886,11 (USD$ 82.048.465, approximately).

Chapter 8. The "JB" Sub-network

J&F Group and Joesley Mendonça Batista: Leading Strategists

Between 2003 and 2017, the J&F Group and its subsidiaries JBS, Eldorado, Florestal, and Vigor, owned by Joesley Mendoça Batista -herein referenced as "JB"- and Wesley Mendoça Batista, established a complex scheme of bribes and money laundering. According to Brazilian prosecutors, the total amount of bribes reached R$ 600 million, approximately USD$ 181,554,000, paid to 1829 politicians from 28 political parties. Judicial sources, such as the statements of Joesley Mendoça Batista and Wesley Mendoça Batista, revealed that through licit and illicit electoral funding, the company influenced the election of its candidates for positions at the Chamber of Representatives, the Brazilian Senate, the governments of four States within the presidency of Dilma Rousseff and Michel Temer.[232]

In this sense, the "JB" sub-network illustrates how nodes/agents in the business and political sectors established agreements through companies and political parties; that explains why this chapter focuses on

---

232 Ministério Público Federal. (2014). *Termo de Pre-Acordo de Colaboracao premiada.* Procuradoria-Geral Da República. Page 65.

understanding agreements between businesspeople – acting through companies– and politicians –acting through political parties. In the long-run, these agreements sustained the overall scheme of macro-corruption that allowed appointing specific officials who favored the scheme in key positions along State companies. With around 89 direct interactions as the active node/agent, and 10 as the passive node/agent, with a darker color in Figure 5 it is clearly observed the key position of Joesley Mendoça Batista, near the nucleus and above of the company JBS.

Figure 5. "JB" located above the company JBS (with a darker color).

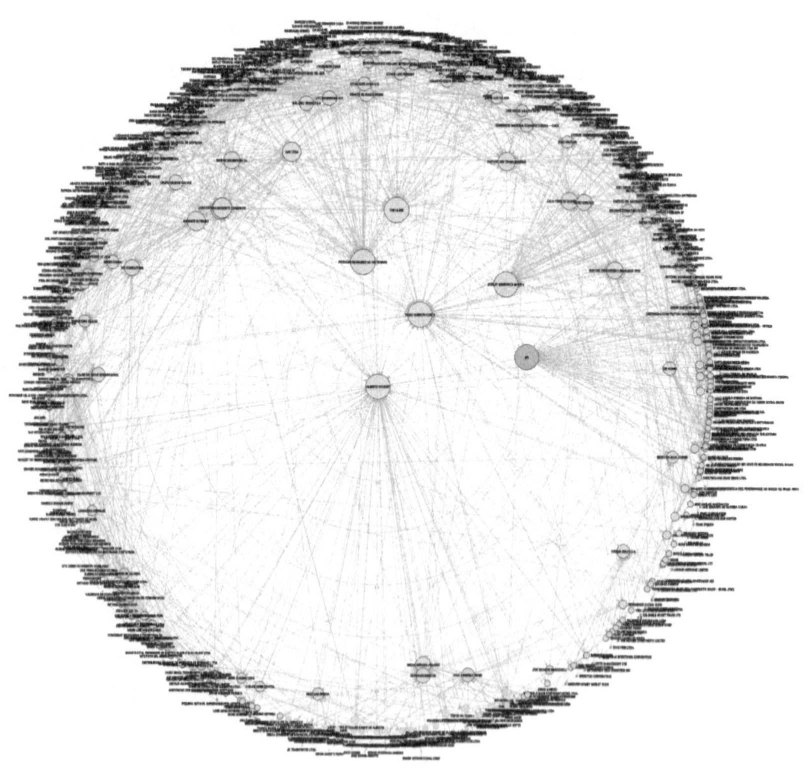

In fact, in Figure 6 it is also observed how "JB" interact directly with political parties such as the *Partido do Movimiento Democratico Brasileiro* (PMDB) and with individuals such as Eduardo Consentino Cuhna, renowed politician. However, the real nature of the scheme of corruption is revealed when considering the indirect interactions established through the company JBS. When removing the "JB" subnetwork outside the overall "Lava Jato" network, it can be noted how Joesley Mendoça Batista used his company to establish a large number of indirect interactions with other companies. As it is explained below, those interactions mostly consisted of contracts between JBS and façade and real companies. In fact, the amount of direct interactions connecting the JBS sub-network with the overall "Lava Jato" structure reaches 271 interactions when counting not only the interactions of "JB" as individual, but also those of the company JBS.

Figure 6. Node/Agent "JB" located above the node/agent that represents the JBS company, highlighted with a darker color.

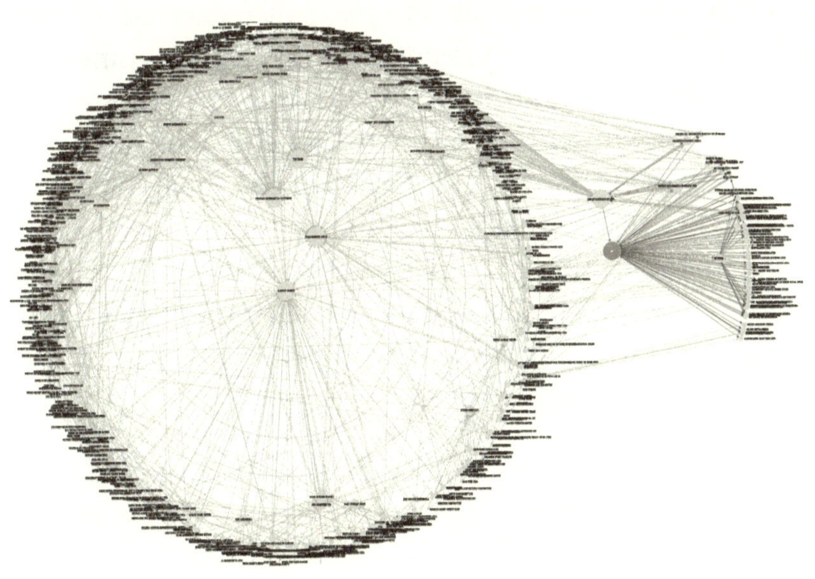

The JB and BNDES Scheme

The first *cliqué* in this sub-network was established in 2004 when JB met Victor Garcia Sandri, a businessman and friend of Guido Mantega, who was *Ministro do Planejamento* at that time. Victor established an agreement with JB to influence Guido Mantega to obtain facilities for JB's companies, in exchange of R$ 50 thousand per month. In 2005, when Guido Mantega became president of the BNDES bank, JBS, a company belonging to the J&F group, submitted 2 loan requests to BNDES for the amount of USD$ 80 million to support the expansion plan of the company. Victor Garcia then asked JB to pay 4% of the the credit to approve the operation. The money received was then transferred through an offshore account owned by JB to another offshore account controlled by Victor García.[233]

Later in 2006, JB continued requesting loans to BNDES with the support of Victor Garcia and Guido Mantega, *Ministro do Fazenda* at that time, who also exerted influence on Luciano Coutinho, president of BNDES. In June 2007, BNDES acquired 12.94% of JBS' shared capital for USD$ 580 million, supporting the company's expansion plan for that year. In exchange, JB paid 4% of the total value of the transaction to an offshore account of Victor Garcia Sandri. Again, in June 2008, BNDES in joint operation with FUNCEF and PETROS acquired an additional 12.99% of JBS' shared capital for USD$ 500 million to support the expansion plan of the company during that year.[234]

Since 2009, JB provided Victor Garcia intermediation and began to negotiate paying commissions directly to Guido

---

233 Ibid. Page 65.
234 Ibid. Page 65.

Mantega. On December 2009, BNDES acquired JBS' share capital for USD\$ 2 billion in support of that year's expansion plan. As payment for this operation, JB requested a loan agreement in favor of Guido Mantega for USD\$ 50 million, deposited in an offshore account allegedly controlled by Luiz Inácio Lula da Silva.[235]

Later, in May 2011, BNDES funded with R\$ 2 billion the construction of a pulp mill for Eldorado company, a subsidiary of J&F group. In return, JB deposited R\$ 30 million (USD\$ 9,077,700 approximately) into an offshore account allegedly controlled by Dilma Rousseff. In 2012, Guido Mantega asked JB to transfer to Pedala Equipamentos Esportivos Ltda. a loan agreement of USD\$ 5 million made by JB through his company Antigua Investments Llc. Then, Pedala closed without having paid back that transfer to JB, who incurred in that loss.[236]

Since 2014, Guido Mantega continued requesting JB to transfer money to accounts of politicians and political parties, registering those transactions as official donations. On the 4th of July, 2014,, Guido Mantega delivered to JB the first list of politicians of the *Partido do Movimento Democrático Brasileiro* (PMDB). Ricardo Saud, J&F's Public Relations Manager, was in charge of the logistics of these transfers. Later that year, a list of politicians who were members of the *Partido dos Trabhaladores* (PT) and received "official donations" by JBS, was provided by Mantega to JB.[237]

---

235 Ibid. Page 66.
236 Ibid. Page 67.
237 Ibid. Page 67.

The JB, BNDES, FUNCEP and PETROS Scheme: Vaccari, Lacerda and Pinheiro as intermediaries

The BNDES scheme extended to obtain funds from PETROS and FUNCEF, enhanced with the participation of the presidents of both funds. In both cases, Guido Mantega determined the participation of JB, the destination of commissions and the percentage of bribes for the presidents of the funds.

During the first half of 2008, BNDES, FUNCEF, and PETROS acquired 12.99% of JBS' share capital for one billion dollars. With this operation BNDES, FUNCEF and PETROS created the fund called PROT to finance the capitalization of JBS.[238]

At that time, Paulo Ferreira was treasurer of the *Partido dos Trabhaladores*, Guilherme Lacerda president of FUNCEF, and Vagner Pinheiro president of PETROS. Guilherme Lacerda introduced JB to Paulo Ferreira, who in turn introduced JB to Joao Vaccari.[239]

Joao Vaccari agreed with JB to influence managers that Vaccari knew would benefit J&F group, in exchange of bribes of 1% for each operation that would benefit J&F, to be paid to the *Partido dos Trabhaladores* party. Simultaneously, JB negotiated with Guilherme Lacerda and Vagner Pinheiro that he would grant them a bribe of 1% of the value of each operation, after establishing PROT.[240]

---

238 Ibid. Page 70.
239 Ibid. Page 70.
240 Ibid. Page 70.

In 2009, FUNCEF and PETROS wanted to invest in reforestation companies, so JB negotiated with Guilherme Lacerda and Vagner Pinheiro to expand Florestal activities as a result of their investment, considering that Florestal was part of the J&F group. Accordingly, the FIP-Florestal fund was created to transfer money, in which FUNCEF and PETROS contributed with approximately R$ 275 million; Mario Celso and his son Mario Celso Lincoln then used the same scheme for their company Eucalipto Brazil. In exchange for that investment, JB paid a commission of 1% of the operation to Guilherme Lacerda and Vagner Pinheiro. For paying those commissions, Guilherme told to JB that these payments would be made through Joao Bosco, a commercial representative in Espírito Santo.[241]

In 2010, Carlos Alberto Caser was appointed as president of FUNCEF, and Luis Carlos Afonso was appointed also as president of PETROS. Both of them continued with the agreement established with JB, initiated by Vagner Pinheiro. In 2011, with the incorporation of Eldorado in FIP-Florestal, JB paid USD$ 1.5 million to Luis Carlos Afonso, through the transfer of an apartment in New York.[242]

From March 2010 to June 2015, JB paid to Vagner Pinheiro through third parties such as Demilton Antonio de Castro and Junior, brother of Vagner Pinheiro, a total of R$ 2,700,841.94 of which R$ 300,000 were paid in cash: R$ 100,000 on February 5th, 2015; R$ 50,000 on March 25th, 2015; R$ 50,000 on May 28th, 2015; R$ 50,000 on June 23rd, 2015; and R$ 50,000 on July 28th, 2015. The remainder was paid through false invoices that Junior

---

241 Ibid. Page 71.
242 Ibid. Page 71.

issued against the J&F group of companies, at a rate of 1% per month, in amounts that began with R$ 34,374.99 and increased progressively until R$ 53,249.99.[243]

The JB and the Chamber of Deputies Scheme: Lucio Funaro and Eduardo Cunha as intermediaries

In 2011, Paulo Sergio Formigoni of Olivera introduced Lucio Funaro to JB. At that time Lucio Funaro already knew that several companies belonging to the J&F group solicited a financial support to *Caixa Econômica Federal* and FI–FGTS. So, during that meeting, Lucio Funaro commented that he had the support of the Vice President, Michel Temer, and the Federal Deputy, Eduardo Cunha, to achieve this objective. Lucio Funaro also added that he could help JB to get funds, as he jointly with Eduardo Cunha were responsible for nominating Fabio Cleto for the position of Vice President of *Fundos de Governo e loterias da Caixa Econômica Federal* [Government and Lotteries Fund, of the Federal Economic Fund]. In exchange for this intermediation, JB had to pay between 3% and 3.5% of the funding obtained. In the same sense, Funaro claimed that he could also access funding from the Caixa Econômica Federal as, together with Eduardo Cunha, he was responsible for nominating Giovanni and Derziê, who held strategic positions at the entity.[244]

Between 2011 and 2014, the operations were carried out through an accounting system that JB created, in which bribes were recorded as invoices issued by the

---

243 Ibid. Page 71.
244 Ibid. Page 72.

J&F group and submitted to companies owned by Lucio Funaro or other companies designated by Funaro.[245]

In July, 2013, Lucio Funaro appointed Rodrigo Figueiredo as *Secretário de Defesa da Agropecuária* and, as a result, Funaro offered a "window of opportunities" to JB's companies[246]. Therefore, JB requested Funaro to obtain the federalization of the animal inspection system in Brazil, considering that the nonfederal character of this system produced market distortions. The requested federalization didn't happen, however, the former deputy Eduardo Cunha tried to obtain a regulation to the exportation of offal, in order to benefit JBS. This regulation was implemented in March 2014, but suppressed in March 2015.[247]

In 2013 JB also asked Funaro to intervene with Rodrigo Figueiredo to revoke the regulations that would allow applying long-lasting *vermifuge*, as a condition to facilitate the exportation of meat. This request was agreed and approved. The bribe for the favorable regulation of the exportation of offal was R$ 2 million (USD$ 615,817.00 approximately), transferred to an account controlled by Lucio Funaro. The bribe for the regulation of long-lasting *vermifuge* was established in R$ 5 million (USD$ 1,539,624.00 approximately) and transferred to an account also controlled by Lucio Funaro. Also, during this period JB paid R$ 400 thousand (USD$ 123,180.00 approximately) monthly in cash through a money carrier, Florisvaldo Caetanio, to the Lucio Funaro' sister, Roberta Funaro.[248]

---

245 Ibid. Page 72.
246 Ibid. Page 72.
247 Ibid. Page 72.
248 Ibid. Page 72.

Between August 2014, and January 2015, Eduardo Cunha ran for the presidency of the Chamber of Deputies and asked JB a commission of R$ 30 million (USD$ 9,236,480.00 approximately) to finance his campaign. Then, JB agreed and the commission was paid with the following transactions: R$ 10,900,000.00 (USD$ 3,354,347.00 approximately) through fake invoices issued by JBS between February 9th and 10th, 2014; R$ 12 million (USD$ 3,692,859.00 approximately) in cash, following the orders of Eduardo Cunha, and R$ 5,600,000.00 (USD$ 1,723,127.00 approximately) through official donations to the PMDB party and several members of the Cunha's evangelic church.[249]

During the period in which Eduardo Cunha became president of the Chamber of Deputies, JB began negotiating directly with him, bypassing Lucio Funaro as an intermediary. In February 2016, Eduardo Cunha requested to JB R$ 20 million (USD$ 6 million, approximately) to distribute among the members of the Chamber, to approve a tax benefit proposal for preserving the payroll exemption to the poultry sector. This bribe of R$ 12 million (USD$ 3,692,019.00 approximately) was paid in cash between March and September 2016, through deliveries from Florisvaldo Caetanio to Altair Alves, with Eduardo Cunha's intermediary.[250]

Another payment of R$ 3 million (USD 922.589 approximately) was delivered by JB himself to Eduardo in suitcases with R$ 1 million (USD$ 307,636.00 approximately), each at the *Jacarepaguá* airport. Additionally, a payment of

---

249 Ibid. Page 73.
250 Ibid. Page 77.

R$ 5 million (USD$ 1,538,490.00 approximately) was delivered in cash after the arrest of Eduardo Cunha, to Altair Alves.[251]

JB and the Presidency: Michel Temer as a Key Active Agent

In 2010, JB met Michel Temer, who at the time was Vice President of Brazil, through Wagner Rossi, the *Ministro do Agricultura* at the moment. During that meeting, JB and Rossi agreed that Temer would support JB for their common interests. Then, in 2010 Michel Temer requested to JB R $3 million (USD$ 923,070.00), registering R $1 million (USD$ 307,644.00 approximately) as official donations and R $2 million (USD$ 615,351.00 approximately) as transactions with the Public Communications Company, through fraudulent invoices. In August and September 2010, Temer requested to JB the payment of R $240 thousand (USD$ 73.884 approximately) to the Island Productions company.[252]

After the departure of Wagner Rossi from the *Ministerio do Agricultura*, Temer requested JB to pay R $100 thousand (USD$ 30,785.00) per month to Rossi and R $20 thousand to Milton Hortolan, who held the position of executive secretary of the portfolio. These payments were delivered during only one year. In 2012, Michel Temer asked JB to pay R$3 million (USD 922.782 approximately) to the electoral campaign of Gabriel Chalita in Sao Paulo. All of these payments were executed through false invoices.[253]

---

251 Ibid. Page 77.
252 Ibid. Page 77.
253 Ibid. Page 78.

During the Dilma's impeachment process, before Michel Temer took over the presidency, Temer himself requested to JB R $300,000.00 (USD$ 92,283.00 approximately) to try to influence the public opinion by bribing mass media companies that attacked him through the internet. This amount was delivered in cash to Elcinho, a publicist of Michel Temer.[254]

Then, when Michel Temer assumed the presidency of Brazil in August 2016, JB and the politician Geddel Vieira Lima established a direct communication channel to receive JB's proposals. In 2016, JB asked Temer, through Geddel, to influence BNDES bank to approve JBS' request for changing its tax domicile abroad, when BNDES had already controlled 25% of the company's capital. In exchange for this request, JB kept Michel Temer informed of the investigation of Eduardo Cunha and Lucio Funaro, and continued paying to keep both of them silent.[255]

After the arrest of Geddel Vieira, JB hired the Federal Deputy, Rodrigo Rocha Loures from the *Partido do Movimento Democrático Brasileiro*, to contact Michel Temer. During that same meeting, JB asked Michel Temer to expedite the approval of amnesties for Caixa 2, analyzed in the previous JB sub-network, and the law of abuse of authority, since the investigations on him were progressing.[256]

---

254 Ibid. Page 78.
255 Ibid. Page 78.
256 Ibid. Page 78.

JB, Politicians and Political Parties

Aecio Neves

In March 2017, Aecio Neves, politician member of the *Partido da Social Democracia Brasilera* requested R$ 2 million to JB, to pay legal advice. In exchange, JB request Aecio Neves to influence on the approval of the law of abuse of authority and amnesty for the Caixa 2 issue. Due to the risk around the investigations in place, the payment was delivered in cash through an emissary of JB to an emissary of Neves.[257]

Antonio Carlos

In 2016, after *Caixa Econômica Federal* approved a loan agreement for R$ 2.7 billion (USD$ 832,198,416.00), the *CEF* Vice President, Antonio Carlos, asked JB to pay R$ 6 million (USD$ 1,849,414.00) to the *Partido Republicano Brasileiro* since his tenure in office had been decided by the influence of Marcos Pereira. The payment was made in cash, in various deliveries of R$ 500 thousand (USD$ 154,114.00 approximately) each one. The total amount paid in the operation was R$ 4,200,000.00 (USD$ 1,294,584.00 approximately), instead of the R$6 million initially requested (USD$ 1,849,414.00 approximately).[258]

---

257 Ministério Público Federal & Procuradoria-Geral Da República. (2017). *Termo de Pre-Acordo de Colaboracao premiada.* Source: http://jud-anexos.digesto.com.br/52619d47af6662e1cc5699929cc151c3.pdf
258 Ibid. Page 93

Antonio Palocci

In 2008, Antonio Palocci, who in 2010 became Dilma's right-hand during her presidential campaign, introduced Antonio Ferreira to JB. At that moment, JB hired Antonio Palocci in order to advise him on the dynamics of Brazilian politics. When they met in 2008, Palocci requested to JB a support of R$ 30 million for the presidential campaign of Dilma; JB agreed and executed the following transfers: R$ 1,820,000.00 paid in cash to Samuel; R$ 612,902.46 paid through 3 fake invoices for *Hedge Assessoria e Consultoria Empresarial*; R$ 1 million in cash delivered to "Gilmarcy"; R$ 16 million as official donations to various candidates nominated by Antonio Palocci.[259]

Marta Suplicy

In 2010, JB met Marta Suplicy, politician of the *Partido do Movimento Democrático Brasileiro*, through Antonio Palocci. In that same year, Marta requested to JB R$ 1 million (USD$ 308,234.00 approximately) to finance her campaign to the Federal Senate. The amount was transferred through an official donation of R$ 500 thousand (USD$ 154,115.00 approximately) and other R$ 500 thousand delivered in cash to Marta Suplicy. Then, in 2015, Marta again asked JB to fund her campaign to the prefecture of Sao Paulo. The money was delivered in cash through Florisvaldo to Marcio, husband of Marta Suplicy. In total, 15 monthly payments for R$ 200 thousand (USD$ 61,646.00 approximately).[260]

---

259 Ibid. Page 93.
260 Ibid. Page 93.

Jose Serra

Joesley Mendoça Batista met Jose Serra during his presidential campaign in 2010, when Serra asked JB donations for his campaign, for a total amount of R$ 20 million (USD$ 6,164,664.00 approximately), transferred as follows: R$ 6 million (USD$ 1,849,399.00 approximately) through fraudulent invoices to the company LRC Eventos e Promoçoes; R$ 420 thousan (USD$ 129,455.00 approximately) to the company APPM Analyst e Pesquisa, also through false invoices; and R$ 13,580.00 (USD$ 4,185.00 approximately) through official donations as the candidate indicated.[261]

Silval Barbosa and Pedro Nadaf

In 2010, Silval Barbosa, governor of Mato Grosso, approached JB soliciting support when running for that office, promising that if winning he would compensate the J&F group of companies by reducing state taxes.[262]

In 2011, Wesley Batista, who replaced JB as president of JBS, began negotiating with governor Sival Barbosa. As a result, Governor Silval Barbosa altered the collection of the Tax of Circulation of Goods and Services ("ICMS"), through the *Decreto Estadual e Convênio CONFAZ*, which benefited JBS's refrigerators in Diamantino. Also, the governor granted to JBS an ICMS credit for R$ 73,563,484.77 (USD$ 22,671,851.00, approximately) registered as compensation for his ICMS payments made under the previous system. Pedro Nadaf, *Secretario da Industria e Comercio*, and Marcel

---

261 Ibid. Page 93.
262 Ibid. Page 95.

Souza de Cursi, *Secretario do Fazenda*, were informed about the agreement. In return for the tax credit, Silval Barbosa requested a commission of R$ 10 million (USD$ 3,082,054.00, approximately) per year, paid in 2012, 2013 and 2014.[263]

During the second half of 2014, the *Secretaria Estadual de Fazenda* inspected and fined JBS for irregularities detected during 2012. The fine reached R$ 180,480,523.67 (USD$ 55,629,838.00 approximately).[264]

In September 2014, the administrative action solicited by Valdir Boni, Silval Barbosa and Pedro Nadaf against the tax inspection carried out in 2014, was rejected, causing losses to the company for more than R$ 74 million (USD$ 22,808,105.00 approximately).[265]

To amend the situation, Pedro Nadaf, *Secretario da Casa Civil* at that time, elaborated a false document stating that PRODEIC was extended in 2012 to all JBS' facilities in the state of Mato Grosso, in order to avoid the payment of the fine. As retribution for the document, Wesley Batista paid Pedro Nadaf and Silval Barbosa the following commissions: (i) R$ 7 million 500 thousand to the company Carol Mila Agropecuaria Ltda., owned by Silval Barbosa, through a surcharge in the purchase of trucks by JBS; (ii) R$ 200 thousand[266] to NBC Consultoria, owned by Pedro Nadaf, through false invoices, (iii) R$ 1 million[267] paid to Trimec through false invoices; (iv) R$ 13 million[268] transferred

---

263 Ibid. Page 95.
264 Ibid. Page 96.
265 Ibid. Page 96.
266 USD$ 61,646.00, approximately.
267 USD$ 308,232.00, approximately.
268 USD$ 4,007,026.00, approximately.

through payments to third parties designated by Pedro Nadaf, (v) R$ 1 million 300 thousand[269] paid to Construtora Sab Ltda. through false invoices, and (vi) R$ 2 million 500 thousand paid in cash through Florisvaldo or Demilton to emissaries of Pedro Nadaf and Silval Barbosa.[270]

Cid Gomes

In 2010, during the re-election of Cid Gomes as governor of Ceará, Arialdo Pinho, *Secretário de Estado of Ceará*, requested JB to pay R$ 5 million (USD$ 1,541,019.00, approximately) for releasing legitimate ICMS credits that the JBS company was supposed to receive from the State.[271] The payment was transferred through official donations and false invoices.

Then, in June 2014, Cid Gomes asked JB and Wesley Batista financial support for Camilo Sobreira de Santana's campaign.[272] Wesley replied that the State of Ceará owed JBS, within the scope of the PROAPI program, R$ 110,404,703.61 (USD$ 34,027,046.00, approximately), and for that reason they would not contribute to his campaign. Subsequently, Federal Deputy, Antonio Balhamann (PROS), together with Arialdo Pinho, proposed to release the ICMS credits in exchange of R$ 20 million (USD$ 6,164,145.00, approximately) for the election campaign, paying R$ 9 million 800 thousand (USD$ 3.020.559, approximately) through

---

269 USD$ 400,684.00, approximately.
270 USD$ 770,566.00, approximately.
271 Ibid, page 98.
272 Ibid, page 98.

false invoices submitted to various companies[273], and R$ 10 million 200 thousand (USD$ 3,143,870.00, approximately) through official donations to various candidates.

Zeca, Andre Puccineli and Reinaldo Azambuja

In 2003, the governor of Mato Grosso do Sul, Zeca, negotiated with JB and offered tax benefits to his companies in exchange for 20% of the total benefits granted. Then, in 2010 Zeca requested JB to pay R$ 3 million (USD$ 924,617.00) for his electoral campaign. As a result, R$ 1 million (USD$ 308,216.00, approximately) were registered as official donations and R$ 2 million (USD$ 616.410, approximately) were delivered in cash.[274]

The following governor, Andre Puccineli, used the same procedure although the paid commission increased to 30% of the benefits. Ivanildo Miranda was the intermediary in charge of receiving the bribes. Then, at the end of Puccineli's government, Andre Luiz Cance passed to be the Puccineli's third party in charge of receiving the bribes, while Valdir Boni was JBS' intermediary. During the government of Andre Puccineli, JBS established five tax benefit agreements with the State of Mato Grosso do Sul: (i) TARE 657/2011, for the extension of slaughtering and deboning activities of the Naviraí branch; (ii) TARE 149/2007, for implementing

---

273 Among the companies that received payments, are: Odola Editorações Ltda., Carlos Pacheco Cinematographic Advisory, Cabuc Computer Graphics Services, Viamar Advertising and Digital Production, Malagueta Cinema e Video Ltda., AMTM Produções Jornalísticas Ltda, M&M Productions Artística Ltda ME, Studio HP of Production and Publicity Creation, Ararema Artistic Production and Publishing, Marche Marketing Ltda., EPP, Helga Thor Production and Editing Ltd., Soufle Imagem e Asuntos Ltda, Communication Opinion, Cankun Institutional Communication, MPC-Marketing Propaganda, N.T. Solver Logística e Serviços Ltda., Ribeiro Neto ME, Síntese Pesquisa e Analise Ltda.
274 Ibid. Page 101.

a refrigerating unit; (iii) TARE 1.028/2014, for expanding the company's activities in the state; (iv) TARE 862/2013, for expanding the company's activities in the state; and (v) TARE 1,103/2016, for expanding and modernizing eight slaughter units in the state.

The company JBS paid a total of R$ 150 million (USD$ 46,238,345.00, approximately) in bribes between 2003 and 2017.[275] This period includes the governments of Zeca, of *Partido dos Trabhaladores* (PT), Andre Puccinelli of *Partido do Movimento Democratrico Brasileiro* (PMDB), and Reinaldo Azambuja of *Partido da Social Democracia Brasileira* (PSDB).

The bribe payments during the government of Andre Puccinelli were made through the intermediaries Ivanildo da Cunha Miranda and Andre Luiz Cance as follow: (i) R$ 5,003,066.00 through false invoices for the purchase of cattle heads, by Ivanildo da Cunha[276], (ii) R$ 9,500,143.00 through false invoices issued by JBS to Protec Construçoes Ltda., (iii) R$ 980 thousand[277] through false invoices issued by JBS to Gráfica Jafar Ltda., (iv) R$ 1,141,250.00[278] through false invoices issued by JBS to MB Produçoes Cinematográficas Ltda., (v) R$ 300 thousand[279] through false invoices issued by JBS to the company Bartz Propaganda Ltda., (vi) R$ 2,834,705.43[280] through false invoices issued by JBS to IBOPE Inteligencia Pesquisa e Consultoria Ltda.,

---

275 Ibid. Page 102
276 Ibid. Page 105.
277 USD$ 302,079.00, approximately.
278 USD$ 351,787.00, approximately.
279 USD$ 92,471.00, approximately.
280 USD$ 873,764.00, approximately.

(vii) R$ 168,109.00[281] through false invoices issued by JBS to Amapil Taxi Aéreo Ltda., (viii) R$ 1,268,850.00[282] through false invoices issued by JBS to Instituto Icone de Ensino Jurídico Ltda., (ix) R$ 22,212.00[283] through false invoices issued by JBS to ST Pesquisa de Mercado Ltda EPP., (x) R$ 2,957,084.95[284] through false invoices issued by JBS to Gráfica e Editora Alvorada Ltda., and (xi) R$ 90 million (USD$ 27,742,388.00, approximately) in cash delivered to third parties according to instructions given by Ivanildo da Cunha Miranda.[285]

Bribe payments during the government of Ricardo Azambuja were made as follow: (i) R$ 12,903,691.03[286], through fraudulent invoices of purchase of beef issued by JBS to Buriti Comercio de Carnes; (ii) R$ 15,497,109.40 (USD$4,776,742.00) through false invoices for the purchase of cattle issued by JBS to third parties: Elvio Rodrigues Rubens Massahiro Matsuda, Agropecuaria Dois Irmas Ltda., Jose Roberto Teixeira, Miltro Rodrigues Pereira, Zelito Alves Ribeiro, Osvane Aparecido Ramos, Francisco Carlos Freire de Oliveira, Nelson Cintra Ribeiro and Marcio Campos Monteiro; and (iii) R$ 10 million (USD$ 3,082,430.00) in cash through third persons indicated by the governor.[287]

---

281 USD$ 873,764.00, approximately.
282 USD$ 391,119.00, approximately.
283 USD$ 6,846.00, approximately.
284 USD$ 911,517.00, approximately.
285 Ibid, page 101.
286 USD$ 3,977,534.00, approximately.
287 Ibid, page 101.

Chapter 9. Institutional Cooptation, Macro-Corruption and Transnational Money Laundering

The illicit network analyzed herein illustrates a highly effective collaboration between private and public sectors to sustain a system of massive corruption in Brazil and transnational massive money laundering, a scheme of effective collaboration that companies such as Odebrecht then replicated across Latin America. Considering the amount and diversity of nodes/agents involved, and the number of resources compromised by this illicit and criminal scheme, this can be interpreted as a case of Institutional Macro-Corruption. In fact, due to the size and complexity of the network, as well as its institutional impacts at the economic, social and political instances, this is one of the most complex cases of the so-called grand corruption to date.

As an outstanding characteristic of the "Lava Jato" illicit and criminal network should be stressed the systematic participation of prominent nodes/agents operating within key lawful private institutions, such as real and front companies. The participation of powerful corporative agents was critical to articulate the network since 72% of the nodes/agents identified in this analysis were private individuals and companies who used their economic power to commit fraud and hide irregular transactions with Petrobras and other State institutions.

Simultaneously, public agents such as former legislative deputies, congressmen and department coordinators at Petrobras were also critical to sustaining the corruption scheme. Those agents used their political power and decision capacity as political leaders and public officials to ally with powerful private agents who supported political parties through electoral campaigns and paid bribes to obtain unjustified favors and advantages in contracts with Petrobras and other State institutions. Furthermore, not only specific individuals but also key positions were co-opted, increasing the resilience of the illicit network and allowing it to replicate itself during several years. In this sense, the scheme not only consisted of sporadic bribes to "buy" or "capture" specific decisions of certain individuals, but of the establishment of a network to reconfigure key institutions to permanently favor illicit purposes.

It is crucial to recognize the decisive role-played by political parties and leading political agents as candidates for the Presidency or for the Congress. In fact, the financial support of political parties and prominent political agents was the main tool used to co-opt political institutions that appointed high-ranking officials who later provided a reciprocal and favorable treatment through legislative initiatives or bureaucratic decisions at public entities under their influence. It cannot be argued that the involved companies were victims of extortion since they actively engaged on paying bribes and requesting benefits, however, they were not the only relevant group of agents who established or benefited from the illicit scheme, since political parties and individual politicians, and high-ranking officials, also engaged actively to establish those agreements, receiving massive payments and benefits. In this sense, any judicial action and public policy reform should address comprehensively all types of agents involved.

Most of the interactions of the network were grouped under the category "Economic" since most of the operations of the "Lava Jato" illicit network involved financial transactions. However, logistic interactions were also important due to the need for coordinating companies, public nodes/agents, and businesspersons for executing financial operations through third parties such as legal representatives of façade companies and transferring money. For example, Nobu Su, former director of Vantage Drilling Corporation and legal representative of Taiwan Maritime Transportation Ltda., paid an undue commission through Oresta Associated S.A. to Hamylthon Padilha, who simultaneously paid to Eduardo Musa and Jorge Luiz Zelade a bribe to facilitate the engagement of Vantage Drilling Corporation, specifically accessing a contract for using the Titanium Explorer –a drill rig ship property of Vantage Deepwater Company. As it can be inferred, the hidden transfer and movement of large amounts of money involving these simultaneous bribes required a skilled and specialized logistic.

This analysis revealed that the companies and public officials involved who participated in the illicit structure used intricate mechanisms and processes to divert, conceal, transfer, and launder money related to unlawful acts. For instance, it was possible to identify that the first layer of bidding companies created a second layer of front companies to transfer money to a third layer of companies established abroad, especially to companies that belonged to public officials who participated in the network. Then, the third layer of companies that initially received money from the second layer of companies, moved it to other offshore accounts that belonged to officials. Therefore, money was transferred among three layers of companies as a mechanism to hinder the possibilities of tracking the sources or the real beneficiaries.

In other cases, officials created front companies to divert money with bogus bids and these, in turn, transferred money to companies abroad. It is important to note that in most of the accounts used to conceal and save money, the owners were sometimes domestic and foreign companies, which allowed hiding the source of assets; however, in some cases, public officials themselves appeared as owners of the companies. An example of this scheme is illustrated through the case of Paulo Roberto Costa, former Supply Director of Petrobras, who held approximate USD$ 23 million in accounts in Switzerland under names of companies such as Aquila Holdings Ltd., Elba Services Ltd., Glacier Finance Inc., International Team Enterprise Ltd., Larose Holding SA, Omega Partners S.A., Quinus Services S.A., Rock Canyon Invest S.A., Sagar Holding S.A., Santa Clara Private Equity, Santa Tereza Services Ltd., Sygnus Assets S.A., and BS Consulting.

Furthermore, according to the evidence analyzed herein, Bernardo Freiburghaus opened several accounts so that Odebrecht could make multiple deposits abroad, every two or three months, directly to Paulo Roberto Costa without paying undue percentage to any political party, by opening accounts in Swiss banks; therefore, there were even tricky and bogus operations to bypass the payment of bribes. As a result, there is evidence of large amounts of money that Odebrecht paid to Diagonal Investimentos owned by Bernardo Freiburghaus, and from the latter to accounts opened in Swiss banks under the name of companies such as Sygnus Assets S.A., Quinus Services S.A., and Sagor Holdings S.A.

In fact, Bernardo Freiburghaus also transferred money between these accounts to ensure that there were no traces that would allow authorities to identify illicit assets; once the funds were transferred between accounts, the account source was canceled. For example, the Quinus Services S.A. account at the HSBC Bank was canceled when its assets were transferred to accounts in the Royal Bank of Canada SA, Banque Cramer & Cia SA, Banquet Pictet & Cia SA, and Pkb Private Bank SA.

From rampant corruption committed through payment of traditional bribes in which money was handed in person, to sophisticated exchange transactions to launder money and the use of several layers of companies, "Lava Jato" reveals various innovative characteristics that should inform stakeholders and enforcement agencies in charge of investigating, prosecuting and sanctioning complex corruption processes like those of institutional co-optation and macro-corruption observed herein.

Some of the most important lessons revealed in this analysis relate to the type of conceptual and technical resources required for understanding and investigating illicit schemes with the complexity revealed. Analysis like the one conducted in this book must be deepened and expanded to provide adequate understanding about the domestic and transnational dimensions, and the scope of these complex networks; otherwise, investigative and enforcement agencies will face these complex corruption phenomena as mere domestic schemes of traditional corruption, impeding the operation of regulatory and judicial institutions and, therefore, increasing penal and moral impunity in the society, and weakening democracy.

Specifically, the complexity observed in the "Lava Jato" network results of (i) the amount and diversity of types of nodes/agents and interactions involved, (ii) the importance of the economic, social and political institutions affected, and (iii) the transnational nature of the entire operation. Addressing this complexity demands innovative conceptual, technical and operational capacities often absent among Attorney General Offices and investigative agencies that traditionally approach and confront corruption as cases of domestic nature, sporadic and isolated. Undoubtedly, investigating, prosecuting and sanctioning networks of institutional co-optation and macro-corruption like the "Lava Jato" illicit network requires transnational articulation and advanced technical capacities at worldwide level; an articulation that does not exist in most regions.

Furthermore, in order to effectively confront institutional co-optation and macro-corruption phenomena, it is required a comprehensive set of reforms at the political, economic, cultural and social spheres, and also determinant societal transformations, as those introduced and discussed in the next chapter.

Chapter 10. Confronting Macro-Corruption: Challenges and opportunities

In 2008, a judicial operation afterwards known as "Lava Jato" happened in Brazil, conceived with the aim of investigating illicit/criminal structures, specifically related to money laundering. The findings derived from this investigation revealed an international corruption network that operated in more than 12 countries. Although information related to the macro-corruption scheme is still confidential in most Latin American countries, the information disclosed by Brazilian authorities allowed understanding the transnational character of the money laundering operations, and the complexity of the domestic network of macro-corruption. These money laundering operations demonstrate that concepts such as national sovereignty, that were highly powerful and relevant until some decades ago, today restrict the field of prosecution and judgment of transnational macro-corruption. Today, more than 40 judicial operations have been developed, revealing more illicit and criminal sub-networks that operate in various structures within the Brazilian corporative, political and public administration systems.

The functioning of these illicit/criminal networks has proven the insufficiency of the concepts and strategies against corruption developed since the 90s. The "Lava

Jato" case is an example of the complexity, scope and systemic nature of illicit/criminal networks that are increasingly articulated by agents operating in a grey zone between legality and illegality, through actions with lawful appearance and under the disguise of legitimacy in legal environments.

According to official sources discussed in the previous chapters and listed in the Annex, the illicit/criminal network unveiled during the Lava Jato operation was articulated by a collusion of powerful companies tightly related with political parties, politicians and high-ranking officials, to provide services to state companies such as Petrobras, Eletrobras, and public institutions for example, the Departments of Health, Public Works, and Transportation of Brazil. Several contracts were monopolized by a group of companies known as "The Club", which through illicit electoral financing, bribery, and influence peddling, manipulated the selection process in a way that these companies won the bids and even, in some cases, these same corporations decided the requirements for tendering. As a result, the participating businesspersons, public officials and political leaders took advantage of their economic and political power and co-opted key institutions to establish a system of macro-corruption.

During the manipulated public tenders, almost every legal requirement was fulfilled only by the colluded companies, providing an appearance of formal legality. Through this method it has been reproduced a system of institutional co-optation and macro-corruption; therefore, reinforcing the benefits of powerful companies, high-ranking state officials and politicians.

Consequently, the system developed an extensive money laundering network to legitimize the assets obtained through bribes and irregular contracts. In this process, the illicit structure used financial operators to divert money into other legal and illegal unrelated businesses through financial funds and accounts held abroad. Façade companies were created and contracts were simulated to simultaneously transfer large amounts of money while maintaining an appearance of legality. These actions usually prevented the authorities from identifying illegal operations, allowing the participating companies, politicians and public officials to accumulate more economic and political power throughout the years. The result of the system of institutional cooptation and macro-corruption was a reconfiguration of certain institutions inside the Brazilian State.

It is clear today that concepts adopted since the last decades have become obsolete to grasp and understand the complexity and scope of the phenomenon herein revealed. On one hand, regarding the traditional concepts of corruption, the "Lava Jato" network did include bribery and manipulation of contracts and public tenders; however, its illicit characters expanded to include massive money laundering at unprecedented levels, while its criminal character also included trafficking activities. On the other hand, regarding the traditional concepts used to define organized crime, "Lava Jato" was not a pyramidal organization: among its 900 nodes/agents, their hierarchies and the resulting flows of resources constantly changed. Additionally, it did not consist only of isolated full-time criminals, but mainly of *grey* agents such as high-rank public officials, key politicians, powerful businesspersons, private companies, and a variety of professionals. It is even difficult to state that there was a single criminal mastermind directing the entire illicit scheme; in fact, there were several sub-networks that sometimes were articulated depending on specific purposes. In this sense, "Lava Jato" is not a traditional criminal organization, but a resilient and complex system of macro-corruption.

Towards a Policy-oriented Framework to Understand and Strategically Confront Decentralized and Transnational Networks of Macro-Corruption and Institutional Co-optation

Adopting a Systemic and Comprehensive Approach

To effectively combat illicit/criminal networks such as those engaged on macro-corruption, massive money laundering and institutional co-optation, it is important to recognize the decentralized character of these networks, reflected in their medium to high level of resilience. As discussed, that resilience results of the fact that these structures do not consists of pyramidal and top-to-down rigid hierarchies in which a single leader concentrates the power of decision; in Lava Jato, as well as other current networks, members of different sub-networks do not necessarily interact each other, at least directly.

In this context, some actions carried out by a sub-network's member can be defined as legal if analyzed from an individual and isolated perspective, but in certain cases, the same actions can be illicit when analyzed in the context of an entire network –through a systemic approach. The convenience and necessity of a systemic approach is even more stressed, for instance, when defining the degree of responsibility of each member in a network and when identifying its operating relevance.

After acknowledging how the main characteristics of current decentralized illicit/criminal networks differ from traditional pyramidal criminal organizations, it is important to adopt new concepts and methodologies for analysis[288]. Consecutively, a legal framework should be adopted to reform and even replace some prevalent approaches and methodologies of investigation, judgment and sanction. Then, those developments should escalate to a transnational level through agreements between Attorney General Offices, for example. As seen in the "Lava Jato" case, the illegal/criminal networks have become sufficiently sophisticated to develop certain activities in specific countries or continents according to the institutional context, for instance, paying bribes in a country, conducting trafficking activities in another and, finally, dissipating assets through third parties in tax havens. This transnational operation is a challenge for conducting effective investigations, prosecutions and judgments, given the legal, jurisdictional and institutional restrictions. As a result, in some countries it is even impossible to unveil the ultimate goals of illicit networks or identify the degrees of responsibility and participation

---

288 Among the most relevant concepts that should be considered and evaluated are: i) hub, which describes the agent within the network that centralizes a large number of direct interactions, ii) structural bridges, which states those agents with highest capacity to manipulate or control flows of information and other resources within the network, and iii) stabilizers, that makes reference to those agents that maintain the cohesion of sub-networks within the network. Through these concepts, and the classification of types of agents and relationships developed in the network, it is possible to embody, in a descriptive way, a technical analysis for the functioning of a network. Through these concepts, it is possible to identify the real level of significance and impact of each agent and its actions.

of all the agents involved. For instance, in the particular case of "Lava Jato" it has been impossible to fully identify the activities of "The Clube" in more than 12 countries were these companies operated even reconfiguring State institutions through illicit political parties supporting, electoral financing and massive bribery.

Unfortunately, prosecutors, attorneys, judicial investigators, judges and journalists usually keep using traditional and insufficient concepts and methodologies when trying to understand this emerging criminal complexity. This situation is aggravated by the lack of institutional arrangements –in the criminal systems– to track and explain the functional relations between transnational and local illicit or criminal dynamics. Although multilateral entities such as the United Nations (UN), the World Bank (WB), the International Monetary Fund (IMF), the Inter-American Development Bank (IDB) and the Organization of American States (OAS) have adopted instruments and protocols to combat corruption in certain regions, their concepts are today obsolete in the context of this increasingly complex and hyper-connected phenomenon.

In fact, the OAS was one of the first multilateral institution that acknowledged the global character of corruption. In 1996 during the Caracas' conference, protocols were approved to prevent and combat corruption. Article VI of the Inter-American Convention against Corruption established five scenarios in which an act can be defined as corrupt[289], while Article VIII established a

---

289 Article VI establishes as governing principles of an act of corruption, the followings: a) solicitation or acceptance, b) offering or granting, c) act or omission, d) fraudulent use or concealment and e) participation.

first scenario in which it is recognized the international character of corruption: "it shall be sanctioned the act of offering or granting to a public servant of a different state, direct or indirectly, by part of their nationals, persons with a habitual residence in its territory and companies domiciled there (...)."[290] This statement reflected a notable progress in terms of understanding and confronting corruption because describing 3 qualifiers for the active node/agent recognizes the existence of illicit transnational networks: it suggests that agreements between 3 active nodes/agents could happen in different territories. This idea is enhanced by the interpretation of Article XI, sections c) and d), which also recognizes an agreement and planning between various subjects to obtain benefits that are strictly economic.[291]

However, although the Inter-American Convention against Corruption acknowledges an agreement between more than 3 individuals, it does not define a comprehensive definition of a complex, transnational and illicit and criminal networks in which hundreds or thousands of agents participate. As a consequence, such restrictive definitions and concepts hinder the analysis to understand

---

290 Article VIII: "Subject to its Constitution and the fundamental principles of its legal system, each State Party shall prohibit and punish the offering or granting, directly or indirectly, by its nationals, persons having their habitual residence in its territory, and businesses domiciled there, to a government official of another State, of any article of monetary value, or other benefit, such as a gift, favor, promise or advantage, in connection with any economic or commercial transaction in exchange for any act or omission in the performance of that official's public functions".

291 Article XI: "... c) Any act or omission by any person who, personally or through a third party, or acting as an intermediary, seeks to obtain a decision from a public authority whereby he illicitly obtains for himself or for another person any benefit or gain, whether or not such act or omission harms State property; and d) The diversion by a government official, for purposes unrelated to those for which they were intended, for his own benefit or that of a third party, of any movable or immovable property, monies or securities belonging to the State, to an independent agency, or to an individual, that such official has received by virtue of his position for purposes of administration, custody or for other reasons.

the effects of the network as whole, and inadequately exclude some nodes/agents and actions openly illegal or at least illegitimate, as they omit the actions of grey agents who are supposedly legal but act in favor of illegal or even criminal interests.[292]

The actions of those grey agents within the private and public sectors who facilitate the development, allocation and further embodiment of biddings must still be understood and explained, since omitting their relevance translates into massive impunity. Traditional concepts that apprehend and explain some acts revealed by the "Lava Jato" operation are still insufficient for explaining some characteristics of the macro-corruption system. In general, given the large amount and diversity of nodes/ agents, institutions, activities and resources flowing across these decentralized and transnational illicit structures, it is important to adopt an integrative and systemic approach to understand the characteristics of macro-corruption and institutional co-optation systems.

Fragmented analysis and investigations and the resulting restricted actions −at criminal, political and social levels− are the most important limitations of the current and prevalent approach, which is also the result of limitations imposed by definitions and protocols enforced by the current criminal codes. Actions executed by nodes/agents of

---

292 For instance, only through an integrative and systemic approach it is possible to understand the role of the companies that allowed Miguel Iskin's firms to establish a fraudulent scheme of international trade of goods and services and international bidding, as the sub-operation "Fratura Exposta" revealed. In the same sense, the "Calicute" and "Saqueador" sub-operations also revealed information concerning an illicit and criminal structure led by Rio de Janeiro's governor, and articulated by his Secretary-General and the representatives of the "The Club" private companies. The banks that played important roles when concealing illegal funds are another example of grey nodes/agents.

illicit/criminal networks are often framed as administrative faults when analyzed from a casuistic approach, and not

from a systemic one. In response to these limitations, it is necessary to recognize and understand the differences between an isolated, pyramidal, vertical and rigid criminal organization articulated by few full-time criminals, and a open, decentralized, horizontal and constantly changing illicit network articulated by various types of nodes/agents who also execute various types of activities that oscillate between illegitimacy, illegality and criminality.

Implementing a Theoretical and Systemic Approach Such as Social Network Analysis (SNA), Including Protocols, Methodologies, and Operative Tools

It is critical that researchers, investigators and judicial operators acknowledge and understand sophisticated and complex forms of corruption that are sometimes omitted in the prevailing criminal codes and legislation.

As it has been discussed in the previous chapters, although it is not the only one, SNA is an adequate conceptual, methodological and operational framework for the empirical study of complex social structures such as systems of macro-corruption and institutional cooptation. Additionally, SNA must be complemented with specific algorithms and protocols in order to rightfully characterize the particular specificities of the referred phenomenon.

The judicial branch should urgently adopt actions to update its investigative and operative capacities in order to effectively analyze and combat macro-corruption and institutional cooptation. Some of those actions are: (i) conducting research to understand the operative and structural characteristics of these illicit and criminal systems at the local and national levels; (ii) conducting international comparative research that deepen on the comprehensive characterization of patterns of transnational macro-corruption; (iii) training and strengthening technical capacities of agencies in charge of investigating and judging corrupt practices and processes; and (iv) constantly analyzing current judicial legislation to promote an iterative update of the criminal and civil codes to facilitate investigating and effectively judging systems of macro-corruption.

Reforming Criminal and Civil Codes to Investigate, Prosecute and Penalize Macro-Corruption

Given the systemic nature of macro-criminal networks, macro-corruption and institutional cooptation, the traditional conventional criminal and civil legislation has been surpassed. As far as in the conventional legislation illicit and criminal actions are defined as committed by one specific agent affecting another agent, and therefore not considered as a system in which responsible agents can be identified, it will be impossible to understand and confront actions that reproduce perverse externalities and negative effects on institutions or even on society as a whole.

The common practice of criminal investigation and prosecution is characterized by a case-to-case approach; as a result, information related to specific illicit or criminal actions are usually isolated between them, even sometimes within an attorney general office.

As mentioned before, in the case of advanced macro-corruption and institutional co-optation it is critical to adopt a comprehensive approach to recognize the systematic character of a large variety of illegitimate, illicit and criminal interactions established among lawful, unlawful and *grey* agents. Therefore, the case-to-case approach must be superseded by a systemic framework.

In this context, the conventional, basic and textbook model of criminal and civil law should be transcended, adopting punishment by deprivation of liberty on actions not only of immediate but also of mediate responsibility, conspiracy or aggravated conspiracy, and illicit or criminal association, in order to guarantee systemic investigations and sanctions to illicit and criminal networks by which there have been materialized multiple unlawful and apparent lawful actions. The extended criminal concept of indirect responsibility and aggravated responsibility in an illicit/criminal network like one of macro-corruption and institutional co-optation, should be incorporated and severely applied under an unquestionable reform of the criminal code.

Complementary, being a critical purpose to recover the public resources unlawfully appropriated, or to compensate the value of the social and private damages, and loss of profits, there should be established in the penal law the application of a legal obligation to effectively pursue asset forfeiture and property confiscation to those nodes/ agents directly or indirectly responsible –individuals and companies– in these macro-corruption networks.

In this context, when the basic case-by-case traditional model of corruption is overcome, transcending towards a systemic understanding of the macro-corruption phenomenon, it is recognized that its most outstanding impacts not only happen at the individual, but also at a macro level, and not exclusively of economic nature; in fact, several infractions executed in the framework of a macro-corruption operation can be classified as typical massive violations of human rights of affected groups of population and society, especially, vulnerable groups.

Consequently, the innovated anti macro-corruption codes should treat some of the social damages under the legal framework developed –domestically as well internationally– to sanction macro-corruption as human rights violations.

Subscribing and Implementing International Cooperation Agreements to Combat Macro-Corruption

Given that macro-corruption is increasingly a transnational phenomenon, it is necessary to define, coordinate and structure common legal and investigative strategies and actions between affected countries. An effective judicial strategy of confrontation should sanction those nodes/agents directly and indirectly involved, responsible for economic, human rights and institutional damages. In fact, it is important to recover public and private resources unlawfully appropriated, confiscating funds and extinguishing façade companies through the application of updated anti money laundering codes.

In this context, criminal and civil criteria should be harmonized at the international level to combat macro-corruption processes at their different instances of action. In this regard, incorporating macro-corruption and institutional co-optation as subjects of universal jurisdiction would facilitate the prosecution and judgment of these systemic crimes. This implies establishing international agreements for exchanging judicial, financial and corporative information among domestic authorities to identify and analyze illicit and criminal actions related to process of macro-corruption at an international level.

Reforming the Institutional Functioning of Political Parties and Electoral Financing

Political parties and political activity in general are currently conceived not just as ideological platforms that represent long-lasting social interests and purposes, but instead progressively as corporative platforms for the unjustified legitimation, imposition and representation of some powerful private, illicit and criminal interests. Political parties are currently used for installing those illegitimate interests at the core of the State institutions, that is, in the public administration across branches and levels. As a result of the illegitimate use of political parties, illicit/criminal networks have constantly compromised –manipulated, captured or co-opted– critical State institutions at the highest levels, distorting the basic principles of the rule of law and the democratic political regime. This is a more advanced and socially perverse stage than the traditional political "clientelism" due to its systemic and corporative nature.[293]

---

293 Garay Salamanca, L. J. (1999). *Construcción de una nueva sociedad.* Bogotá: Tercer Mundo Editores-Cambio.

Therefore, it is necessary to reform the functioning and institutional architecture of political parties to guarantee that they represent and promote ideological platforms, propose programmatic social agendas, reinforce deliberative participation, promote new political leaderships, incorporate excluded groups to the political deliberation, act as promoters of long-lasting public interests over egoistic individual private interests, and contribute to strengthen the development of democracy and the democratic regime.

In general, electoral financing facilitates institutional co-optation and the discriminatory influence of powerful private, illicit and criminal interests into public administration, public biddings and contracting to guarantee unjustifiable treatment to those colluded private agents involved. In spite of their own limitations, it is therefore critical to adopt protocols and technological tools by prosecutors and judges, to understand functional relations between political, private and illicit/criminal structures, as the SNA already mentioned; it is also critical to establish task forces to improve judicial investigation against illicit funding, reinforcing both criminal and administrative sanctions against unlawful electoral funding by enforcing strict and comprehensive regulation codes on donations and sponsorships.

In order to address the participation of publicly elected officials in macro-corruption networks, it is important to complement the previously mentioned sanctions – regarding direct and indirect responsibility in illicit and criminal systems– with administrative and political sanctions enforced not only at the level individuals but also of political parties and movements. To confront these processes of macro-corruption and institutional cooptation through electoral financing, it has been commonly proposed to eliminate the private financing of political parties and electoral campaigns. Although this reform would contribute to ameliorate the phenomenon, it would not prevent all the perverse consequences resulting of the discriminatory collusion established by private and corporative interests and powerful politicians. Therefore, strict monitoring and sanctions are needed to investigate and penalize political parties and movements.

Applying Early Warning Systems for Detecting Illicit and Criminal Networks of Macro-Corruption

Recently, early warning systems have been implemented in some European countries to prevent corruption activities and to identify illicit and criminal networks, therefore, contributing to identify risk areas in which those networks tend to operate. This information is critical to prevent opportunities for corruption and constantly provide inputs not only for enforcement reaction but also for preventive public policy. Some main areas in which permanent preventive monitoring must be adopted to identify malpractices, are: key State institutions that concentrate economic or political power, corporative activities, political party administrations, and electoral campaigns. The resulting information should be useful for activating support lines and task forces to follow-up citizen reports and expert analyzes.

Institutionalizing Judicial Sub-Systems Specialized on Judging Cases of Macro-Corruption and Institutional Co-Optation

The Peruvian experience during and after the Fujimori's regime shows how critical it was in 2000 to establish an anti-corruption judicial sub-system for advancing on prosecutions, assets recovery and enforcing punishments to the members of the network of corruption and other illicit activities under the leadership of Montesinos and Fujimori.[294] Therefore, specialized judicial sub-systems will be a key element for strengthening capacities for investigating, prosecuting and judging macro-corruption and institutional co-optation in several countries.

An anticorruption sub-system, composed by highly trained investigators and judges, must operate under favorable organizational conditions and autonomy, which was critical in Peru for conducting appropriate legal actions against Montesinos under the crimes of corruption, money laundering and illicit enrichment, and finally against the president Fujimori himself. As the "Lava Jato" case has revealed, it is highly difficult to investigate, prosecute and judge cases of macro-corruption when executed under "apparent" legal conditions.

Therefore, it is necessary to strength the capacities of judges and other officials at the anti-corruption sub-system in charge of investigating macro-corruption and institutional co-optation. It is especially important to improve technical and institutional capacities to apply innovative criminal and administrative procedures and

---

294 Salcedo-Albarán, E., & Garay Salamanca, L. J. (2016). *Macro-criminalidad: Complejidad y Resiliencia de las Redes Criminales*. Bloomington: iUniverse.

sanctions. In this regard, it is also important to adopt specific protocols to manage, systematize and analyze large amounts of information, since investigating, prosecuting and judging macro-corruption processes will consist of understanding a large amount of agents, types of relationships and sub-networks.

Strengthening Administrative Investigations and Sanctions to Prevent the so-called "Revolving Door"

In various countries it is common that after serving as officials in key regulatory and administrative positions, individuals then work in the private sector to provide their expert knowledge on how to strategically avoid administrative or legal requirements, and on how to obtain unjustified exclusive benefits. Although some countries have adopted disciplinary codes to prevent this phenomenon known as "revolving door" between regulatory agencies and corporations, those entities in charge of enforcing that code usually lack the capacities for executing the detailed investigations required, as well as for and imposing the established sanctions. Therefore, especially in Latin American countries with weak, it is critical establish also sub-systems inside those entities, with the methodological and technological capacities for investigating and enforcing administrative sanctions in cases of violations of inabilities and conflicts of interests at the public administration.

Applying a Risk Oriented Approach to Detect Money Laundering Resulting of Macro-Corruption Networks Through Real Time Analysis of Illicit Financial Flows

The primary and most basic goal of traditional and simple corruption is to generate economic profits. Therefore, money laundering is an illicit activity closely related to corruption in any stage, especially when that corruption becomes systemic.

The primary objective of money laundering processes, as often asserted, is to convert money derived from illicit transactions –which is "dirty"– into other legitimate assets, thereby concealing the predicate transaction. International law[295] has therefore urged governments to criminalize money conversion processes. In fact, countries are required to penalize the laundering of illicit funds derived from activities that happen within their territory, as well as illicit funds originating abroad. In addition, attention should be paid to proceeds generated by local crime and transferred to foreign countries. However, several *grey* areas continue to afflict the criminalization of money laundering around the world. Uncertainty is centered around the lack of uniformity on which predicate transactions are illicit, except for activities recognized by international criminal law, such as drug trafficking. Therefore, the development of a common criminal law around money laundering has been modest, especially when related to corruption.

---

295 International instruments with guidelines to confront money laundering are the UN Convention Against Transnational Organized Crime (2000); Council of Europe Convention on Laundering, Search, Seizure and Confiscation of the Proceeds from Crime and on the Financing of Terrorism (1990); the Money Laundering and Financial Crimes Strategy Act (1998); and the UN Convention Against Corruption, 2003.

Although instruments such as the OAS Convention Against Corruption and the UN Convention Against Transnational Organized Crime have been brought into existence to advance a convergence and harmonization of domestic criminal laws against corruption, the level of domestic application is still uneven between countries.

Anti–Money laundering strategies and laws rely heavily on identifying "suspect" transactions. By definition, compliance legislation can only work where and when there is solid evidence for suspicion. The existence of such evidence is based on background information and the identification of certain activities that are more propitious or more vulnerable to money laundering. A starting point for identifying different money laundering activities, therefore, consists on locating predicate activity areas from which proceeds related to money laundering are derived. Potentially, there are as many activities relevant to inquiry as there are varieties of economic crimes. For that reason, it is necessary to prioritize activities based on the perceptions of law enforcement authorities. For example, the American origin of the term "money laundering" is intricately connected to organized crime in the activities of alcohol trafficking and prostitution. When it was introduced into international criminal law, money laundering control was directed to drug trafficking[296]. In many ways, syndicated drug trafficking is still regarded as a core predicate activity for money laundering. However, since early 80s the drug trafficking industry has been known to influence trends in

---

296 Goredema, C. (2004). *Money laundering in Southern Africa. Incidence, magnitude and prospects for its control.* Institute for Security Studies Papers, 2004(92), p. 11.

"downstream" crimes, notably vehicle theft, smuggling, corruption, housebreaking, armed robbery and murder.

In this sense, protocols must be established to identify suspicious transactions derived from legal activities but potentially useful for money laundering and to understand the potential social structures in which assets are hidden. An updated regional criminal networks database shall exist, centralizing data about domestic and transnational illicit structures. International experience has proven that effective disruption of criminal networks can only be achieved, among other factors, when strategies are preceded and informed by intelligence, and corruption is not an exception. In fact, intelligence analysis becomes even more relevant considering that macro-corruption at the domestic level usually involves cash movements or the use of third parties to hide illicit assets, which means that it is critical for money laundering authorities being able to understand the social structure of the social agents involved.

Since analysis transform raw data into intelligence, it is necessary to adopt processes, protocols, methodologies and technological tools to be executed on a permanent basis. Without the ability to perform an effective and real-time analysis, the intelligence process is reduced just to a simple storage and retrieval system of unrelated data. The increasing volume of global transmitted data that informs about illicit financial flows imposes the need of permanent and real-time analysis.

Protocols related to Social Network Analysis (SNA) are currently critical for visualizing and understanding illicit financial flows between social agents, individuals and groups. These protocols allow authorities to concentrate their efforts on those agents who play a role of stabilization of the illicit and criminal structures.

It is also important to consider the increasing use of crypto-currencies –such as Bitcoin, Ethereum, Ripple, Cardano, EOS, among others– for new means of exchange and as units of value, creating an unprecedented favorable environment for massive money laundering at global scale. Specifically, the *blockchain* technology used to sustain the operation of these crypto-currencies makes them secure at registering each transaction but in theory practically untraceable. The perverse potential consequences in terms of reinforcing and expanding money laundering related to transnational macro-corruption and institutional co-optation, at this stage should be confronted through deep research in order to develop tools that allow a strict regulation of the emission and monitoring of these currencies. This is a new area of international public policy and regulation that should be developed as a priority in the immediate future.

Implementing Innovative Judicial Controls and Complementary Administrative Controls on Public Contracting Processes

As revealed by "Lava Jato", some types of illicit and criminal interactions between public and private agents materialize through the tenders and execution of public contracts. Some penal, administrative and organizational actions that should be comprehensively and complementary implemented to effectively reduce risks of corruption in contracting processes, are: (i) Defining and applying a reduced number of well specified types of contractual models to promote free competition between bidding companies and to guarantee an equitable distribution of risks between the parties involved; (ii) real-time monitoring of information related to public contracting processes through teams entrusted to conduct: preventive monitoring of calls for tenders, analysis of accomplishments of bidding companies that have participated in previous public contacting processes, background checking of companies' representatives, comparative analysis of prices; (iii) monitoring and assessment of amendments to public contracts, enforcing a strict verification of incremental costs and opportune reporting of modifications to the corresponding Attorney General Office; and (iv) providing wider access to information and control over public expenditures and State contracting through effective system of accountability at the local and national levels of administration.

Implementing Political, Criminal and Administrative Controls and Sanctions to Unlawful Transactions and Lawfully Apparent Appropriations in Fragile and Highly Risky Markets

As a general principle, to design an anti-corruption strategy it is necessary to conduct a risk analysis of the markets that are vulnerable to reproducing unlawful or apparently lawful transactions. Illicit/criminal networks will tend to operate in these fragile and vulnerable markets by investing the resources generated through illegal activities. This analysis will allow identifying the most adequate norms, regulations and controls to prevent activities susceptible of being reproduced in each selected risky market, according to its corresponding particular characteristics.

One distinguished risky market is the land market in countries characterized by *"extractive rentism"* as a social agrarian regime –much deeper and structural than the traditional "rent seeking" behavior–[297], being the land more a kind of military, political and social asset than a pure economic-investment asset ruled not by just its economic profitability but specially by its usefulness to accumulate power in general.

Bearing this in mind, a well-known case is institutional co-optation of the State that happened in Colombia during the last three decades, which resulted in more than 7 million

farmers displaced from their lands through violence and political agreements executed by guerrillas, paramilitaries, drug traffickers, local and regional politicians, high-ranking elected officials as local mayors, departmental governors and national congressmen. Consequently, more than 7 million of hectares were abandoned or usurped. A proportion of these lands were illegally appropriated by illicit/criminal networks, first by the victimizers themselves, and then resold through apparent lawful transactions to third parties, especially powerful landowners and private companies who knew the antecedents of violence and massive forced displacement of farmers in the corresponding regions.

---

297 Garay Salamanca, L. J. (1999) *Construcción de una nueva sociedad*. Tercer Mundo Editores-Cambio, and Garay Salamanca, L. J. (2014). "Sobre la problemática de la propiedad y el uso de la tierra en un contexto de usufructo del poder y la violencia como en Colombia. A propósito de algunas perspectivas clásicas de economía política". Bogotá, agosto (recently published, March 2018, as Working Paper by Vortex Foundation).

Strengthening Accountability and Institutional Transparency Through Advocacy and Civic Organizations

Accountability remains as one of the most important mechanisms to control and confront basic modalities of

corruption. In fact, it has been found that in countries with repressive legislation that restrict media freedom, acts of corruption receive less attention and, therefore, are not effectively addressed. Furthermore, at least for the United States, it has been found that isolated cities with low level of media and civic scrutiny are more prone to corruption.[298] Also, after reviewing the situation of corruption and media legislation in Mexico, it was found out that "when the reputation of well-positioned actors like politicians and bureaucrats is at stake, the threat of judicial prosecution is sufficiently credible to have an observable –both statistically and substantially significant– deterrence effect on the behavior of reports and editors".[299]

Despite the sophistication of transnational macro-corruption and institutional co-optation, bribery remains as a common mechanism for consolidating the basic operation of the scheme. However, although bribery, especially the one paid by foreign firms, is commonly accepted as a perverse tool with negative effects on the society and for the business environment, it has also been argued that

---

[298] Campante, F. R., & Quoc-Anh, D. (2014). *Isolated Capital Cities, Accountability, and Corruption: Evidence from US States.* **The American Economic Review,** 104(8), pages 2456-2481.
[299] Stanig, P. (Jan. de 2015). *Regulation of Speech and Media Coverage of Corruption: An Empirical Analysis of the Mexican Press.* **American Journal of Political Science,** 59(1), 175-193. page 191.

bribery is nothing more than an inevitable transaction cost for businesses.

For instance, during the debates around the enactment of the "Foreign Corrupt Practices Act" (FCPA) in 1977, in the United States it was argued that bribes "were simply a cost of doing business abroad and the failure to provide them could put U.S. firms at a competitive disadvantage." Although these debates happened four decades ago, similar approaches are still common, implying that transparency enforced by the FCPA is a disadvantage for United States firms that globally face competition against Chinese and Russian companies in which transparency is irrelevant or negligible, especially when operating "in developing countries where corruption is often the widespread".[300] In fact, during the 60s it was also suggested that "corruption could assist development by facilitating capital information and hence investment".[301]

These arguments explain why in some countries accountability and anticorruption norms are sometimes pointed out as a cause of economic crisis that follows corruption scandals; it is sometimes argued that modifying the corrupt *status quo* causes economic crisis, and not the corruption itself. In countries like Guatemala, actions against the corrupt *status quo* are often defined as left-wing efforts for destabilizing the country. In Brazil, the investigations against Lula have also sometimes been defined as political prosecution.

In contrast, the most recent empirical evidence provided by Lippitt suggests that the enforcement of the FCPA has

---

300 Lippitt, A. H. (2013). *An Empirical Analysis of the Foreign Corrupt Practices Act. Virginia Law Review*, 99(8), 1893-1930. page 1986.
301 Williams, R. (1999). *The New Politics of Corruption. **Third World Quarterly***, 20(3), 487-489. Page 487.

improved the global combat against corruption: "countries with greater numbers of prosecuted FCPA violations also tend to be those where people perceive corruption to be declining". At the end, the commonly accepted approach today is that transparency is critical for improving an environment for fair business competition.[302]

Unfortunately, in spite of the recognized importance of strengthening conventional institutional transparency and accountability, it should be stressed that its effectiveness diminishes substantially when confronted to a systemic, multi-level and trans-national phenomenon such as the institutional co-optation and macro-corruption one. As a countervailing factor, accountability needs to be reinforced not only by a conscious, informed and pro-active citizenship, but very important by a compromised expert contribution to understand the technical and technological characteristics and implications of a complex and updated phenomenon as the macro-corruption and institutional co-optation one.

Legitimating and Renewing Foundational Societal Principles

As it has been discussed, when criminality and corruption become systemic and acquires a transnational and multi-level dimension, then complex and comprehensive legal, regulatory and administrative approaches should be adopted. Furthermore, in order to prevent, confront and even reverse the phenomenon of corruption it is required to formulate and adopt a renovated civic, political, social, cultural and moral heuristic that supersedes the traditional one; this includes renewing civic values, social rules and

---

302 Ibid. Page 1928.

norms, regulations and institutions in anomic societies where illegality remains at the core of their values.

In these sense, after recognizing the need and importance of the reforms and innovations required at various social levels, it should be clear that as more advanced the macro-criminality and macro-corruption phenomenon, *ceteris paribus*, deeper the foundational nature of the societal changes required.[303]

Various foundational principles must be comprehensively legitimated and adopted at social level, some of which are listed below as illustrative exemplification, since their detailed analysis is not the main purpose of this book.

Legitimating the Prevalence of the Public Sphere and the Rule of Law

It should be reproduced an inclusive societal process for reinventing the public sphere in order to guarantee a due observance of the public interests and the human rights of the general population and not only of those with more economic and political power and capacities; this observance should also be adopted according to human progress and sustained by international consensus. This requires, among others, to develop a renovated civic culture transcending the citizen's accountability role and advancing towards a participative and deliberative role to de-construct the private-public relationships under a *"societal individualistic"*

---

303 Garay Salamanca, L.J. (1999). *Construcción de una nueva sociedad.* Tercer Mundo Editores-Cambio, y Garay Salamanca, L. J. (2002). *Repensar a Colombia.* Bogotá: Alfaomega.

heuristic that transcends the *"individual individualistic"* one.[304]

A societal principle underlined here due to its relevance to confront corruption, is the one related to the prevalence of main public interests over egoistic and excluding ones, especially those powerful imposed as result of unjustified privileges obtained through illicit or even criminal practices, such as corruption or even violence. Therefore, it is required to dismantle the societal roots of the so-called *"excluding rentism"*, adopted as a prevalent form of interaction in many societies.[305]

It is worth to stress the key societal role and compromise that should be assumed by political parties, the media and corporative leaders among other leading sectors of society, to promote transparency and accountability of those activities that have a broad social impact. Moral scrutiny should be ineludible among elite's actions and decisions of political sphere. It is important to enforce moral rejection to illegality and formal lawfulness, to publicize acts and processes of corruption, illegality and criminality in general, and to defend the prevalence of the Rule of Law.

---

304 Garay Salamanca, L. J. (1999). *Construcción de una nueva sociedad.* Tercer Mundo Editores-Cambio, y Garay Salamanca, L. J. (2000). *Ciudadanía, lo público, democracia. Textos y notas.* Litocencoa. Bogotá.
305 Garay Salamanca, L. J. (1999). *Construcción de una nueva sociedad.* Tercer Mundo Editores-Cambio.

A Societal Renovation of a Culture of Legality and a Societal Regulation of Markets in a Competitive System

Corruption is not only explained by the possibility of obtaining economic benefits, but under certain circumstances, by an insufficient "moral cost or moral rejection/penalization" imposed by the society to the agents responsible of committing unlawful, illicit or criminal acts[306]. In general, the precarious moral penalization diminishes the confidence and co-responsibility in defense of the Rule of Law and the prevalence of public interests, creating a propitious environment for illegality and unlawfulness.

Consequently, it is necessary to renovate a societal foundational pact to promote and impose a culture of legality and lawfulness, as a pre-condition to effectively combat social and deep-rooted illicit and criminal processes such as macro-corruption and institutional co-optation.

Additionally, the prominent interference and distortive role of powerful private interests in the functioning of the political system, and the consequent reproduction of illegality, perversely impacts the foundations of the market regime, as it was mentioned in the first Chapter. Hence, the social bases for reproducing "equitable competitive markets" should be instituted under the societal principles of equity, confidence, reciprocity, and transparent competition, according to the prevailing capitalist market system by constitutional mandate.

---

306 Pizzorno, A. (1992). "La corruzione nel sistema político" Introduzione a della Porta. *Lo Scambio Occult*. Bologna: Il Mulino.

A Societal Vindication of Politics in a Democratic Regime

As mentioned in the first Chapter, an advanced co-optation of the State by powerful egoistic and excluding private interests –especially if it is under a kleptocratic corporative system– tends to fragment the political system, and to weaken the due observance of the Rule of Law and the legitimation of the State. As a result, depending on how advanced the institutional co-optation and macro-corruption are, it is important to rebuild the legitimacy of politics and political parties, and the social representation of the State.

In this sense, confronting systems of macro-corruption and institutional co-optation should be stressed as a social priority through the vindication and legitimation of *politics* as a collective space for representing and deliberating social interests and purposes through social deliberation and dialogue. This social dialogue will allow renovating the political regime, the deliberative participation and the

consolidation of democracy.[307] This, obviously, implies structural transformations of the prevalent *raison d'être* of politics and of the determinant role that some key political parties are playing in many countries around the world to promote powerful egoistic and excluding interests, even in some cases unlawful, illicit and criminal interests, at the expense of collective long-lasting purposes. It is critical that powerful elites reject and supplant the economic, cultural and political logic and rationale that unleashed processes of macro-corruption

---

307 Garay Salamanca, L. J. (2002). *Repensar a Colombia*. Bogotá: Alfaomega.

and institutional co-optation, in accordance with basic collective principles such as the prevalence of the Rule of Law and the public sphere, the vindication of the State and the legitimation of the deliberative democratic regime.

Bibliography

Almeida dos Santos, R., de Hoyos Guevara, A. J., Sanches Amorim, M. J., & Ferraz-Neto, B. (2012). Compliance and leadership: the susceptibility of leaders to the risk of corruption in organizations. *Einstein (São Paulo) vol.10 no.1*.

Azevedo Sodré, A., & Colaço, M. F. (2010). Relação entre Emendas Parlamentares e Corrupção Municipal no Brasil: Estudo dos Relatórios do Programa de Fiscalização da Controladoria-Geral da União. *RAC - Revista De Administração Contemporânea*, 414-433.

Bagashka, T. (2014). Unpacking Corruption: The Effect of Veto Players on State Capture and Bureaucratic Corruption. *Political Research Quarterly*, 67(1), 165 - 180.

Barua. (2016). Brazil: Yearning for the good times, Global Economic Outlook, Q2 2016. *Deloitte University Press*.

Batista, M. (2013). INCENTIVOS DA DINÂMICA POLÍTICA SOBRE A CORRUPÇÃO. Reeleição, competitividade e coalizões nos municípios brasileiros. *Revista Brasileira de Ciências Sociais*, 87-106.

Batista, M. (2013). INCENTIVOS DA DINÂMICA POLÍTICA SOBRE A CORRUPÇÃO. Reeleição, competitividade e coalizões nos municípios brasileiros. *Revista Brasileira de Ciências Sociais*, , 87-106.

BBC. (July 12, 2017). El expresidente de Brasil Lula da Silva, condenado a 9 años y medio de prisión por corrupción y lavado de dinero. *BBC*. Source: https://goo.gl/joxnW9

Bedinelli, T., & Benites, A. (May 25, 2017). Las protestas contra el presidente Temer paralizan el Gobierno de Brasil. *El País*. Source: https://elpais.com/internacional/2017/05/24/actualidad/1495652623_766724.html

Boas, T., Hidalgo, F., & Richardson, N. (2014). The Spoils of Victory: Campaign Donations and Government Contracts in Brazil. *The Journal of Politics 76(02)*. Source: https://www.researchgate.net/publication/267796197_The_Spoils_of_Victory_Campaign_Donations_and_Government_Contracts_in_Brazil

Campante, F. R., & Quoc-Anh, D. (2014). Isolated Capital Cities, Accountability, and Corruption: Evidence from US States. *The American Economic Review*, *104(8)*, 2456-2481.

Carson, L., & Mota Prado, M. (2014). Mapping corruption and its institutional determinants in Brazil. International Research Initiative on Brazil and Africa . *(IRIBA) Working Paper: 08.* .

Dávid-Barrett, E., & Philip, M. (2015). Realism About Political Corruption. *Annual Review of Political Science*, 387-402.

den Bossche, P. V., & Segers, M. (2013). Transfer of training: Adding insight through social network analysis. *Educational Research Review, 8*, 37-47.

El País. (March 31, 2006). El Congreso brasileño pide el procesamiento de decenas de políticos. *El País*. Source: https://elpais.com/diario/2006/03/31/internacional/1143756016_850215.html

Ferraz, C., & Finan, F. (2011). Electoral Accountability and Corruption: Evidence from the Audits of Local Governments. *American Economic Review, 101(4)*.

Filgueiras, F., & Aranha, A. (2011). Controle da

corrupção e burocracia da linha de frente: regras, discricionariedade e reformas no Brasil. *Dados, 54.*

Flynn, P. (2005). Brazil and Lula, 2005: crisis, corruption and change in political perspective. *Third World Quarterly,* 26(8), 1221-1267(47). Source: https://doi.org/10.1080/01436590500400025

Folha de Sao Paulo. (Dec 22, 2016). Odebrecht Group Paid Out US$ 1 Billion in Bribes in 12 Countries, Says USA. Source: https://www1.folha.uol.com.br/internacional/en/brazil/2016/12/1843856-odebrecht-group-paid-out-us-1-billion-in-bribes-in-12-countries-says-usa.shtml

Gallas, D. (March 7, de 2017). Brazil's Odebrecht corruption scandal. *BBC News.* Source: http://www.bbc.com/news/business-39194395

Garay Salamanca, L. J. (1999). *Construcción de una nueva sociedad.* Bogotá: Tercer Mundo Editores-Cambio. Bogotá.

Garay Salamanca, L. J. (2000). *Ciudadanía, lo público, democracia. Textos y notas.* Bogotá: Litocencoa.

Garay Salamanca, L. J. (2002). *Repensar a Colombia.* Bogotá: Alfaomega. Bogotá.

Garay Salamanca, L. J. (2014). "Sobre la problemática de la propiedad y el uso de la tierra en un contexto de usufructo del poder y la violencia como en Colombia. A propósito de algunas perspectivas clásicas de economía política". Bogotá, agosto (recently published, March 2018, as Working Paper by Vortex Foundation).

Garay Salamanca, L. J., Salcedo Albarán, E., de León Beltrán, I., & Guerrero, B. (2008). *La Captura y Reconfiguración Cooptada del Estado en Colombia.* Bogotá: Grupo Método.

Garay Salamanca, L. J., & De León Beltrán, I. (2009).

From State Capture towards the Co-opted State Reconfiguration: An Analytical Synthesis. Bogotá: Método.

Garay Salamanca, L. J., Salcedo-Albarán, E., & De León Beltrán, I. (2010). *Illicit Netoworks Reconfigurating States: Social Network Analysis of Colombian and Mexican Cases.* Bogotá: Metodo Foundation.

Garay Salamanca, L. J., & Salcedo-Albarán, E. (2012). *Narcotráfico, Corrupción y Estados.* Bogotá: Debate.

Garay Salamanca, L. J., & Salcedo-Albarán, E. (2015). *Drug Trafficking, Corruption and States: How Illicit Netoworks Shaped Institutions in Colombia, Guatemala and México.* iUniverse.

Gray, H. S. (2015). The political economy of grand corruption in Tanzania. *African Affairs, 114*(456), 282-403.

Harrison, E. (2007). Corruption . *Development in Practice,* 672-678.

Hellman, J. S., Jones, G., & Kaufmann, D. (2000). *"Seize the State, Seize the Day" State Capture, Corruption, and Influence in Transition.* The World Bank.

Hellman, J., & Kaufmann, D. (2001). Confronting the Challenge of State Capture in Transition Economies. *Finance & Development, 38*(4).

Hérmida, X. (May 19, 2017). El Supremo de Brasil coloca a Temer al borde de la destitución. *El País.* Source: https://elpais.com/internacional/2017/05/18/actualidad/1495118590_847067.html

Hipólito, M. (2016). Democracy in Brazil: Has anything changed since the early 1990s? *Latin American Research Centre.* Source: https://larc.ucalgary.ca/publications/democracy-brazil-has-anything-changed-early-1990s

Johnson, J. A., R. J., Norwood, B. F., McCoy, D. M.,

Cummings, B., & Tate, R. R. (2013). *Social Network Analysis: A Systematic Approach for Investigating.* FBI Law Enforcement Bulleting.

Jusbrasil. (2010). Doze partidos têm histórico de "mensalões". *Jusbrasil.* Source: https://oab-ma.jusbrasil.com.br/noticias/2027976/doze-partidos-tem-historico-de-mensaloes

Kaufmann, D., Kraay, A., & Mastruzzi, M. (2010). *The Worldwide Governance Indicators: Methodology and Analytical Issues.* The World Bank.

Kaufmann, D., Kraay, A., & Mastruzzi, M. (September 24, 2010). The Worldwide Governance Indicators: Methodology and Analytical Issues. *World Bank Policy Research Working Paper No. 5430.*

Lawrence, L. (2013). Corrupt and Unequal, Both. *Fordham L. Rev, 83*(2). Source: http://ir.lawnet.fordham.edu/flr/vol84/iss2/4

Lessig, L. (2013). "Institutional Corruption" definend . *Law Med,* 2-4.

Lippitt, A. H. (2013). An Empirical Analysis of the Foreign Corrupt Practices Act. *Virginia Law Review, 99*(8), 1893-1930.

Lopes, E. (2010). As gramáticas morais da corrupção: aportes para uma sociologia do escândalo. *Teoria Política e Social na Contemporaneidade,* 126-147.

Martínez García, D. (2014). La Corrupción y su efecto retroalimentativo: Una de las mayores amenazas a la democracia. *Letras Jurídicas*(29), 107-118.

Ministério Público Federal & Procuradoria-Geral Da República. (2017). *"Termo de Pre-Acordo de Colaboracao premiada".* Source: http://www.mpf.mp.br/para-o-cidadao/caso-lava-jato/desmembramentos/rio-de-janeiro/documentos/sentenca-radioatividade

Ministério Público Federal & Procuradoria-Geral Da República. (2017). *Termo de Pre-Acordo de Colaboracao premiada.* Source: http://jud-anexos.digesto.com.br/52619d47af6662e1cc5699929cc151c3.pdf

Ministério Público Federal & Procuraduria da República no Estado do Rio de Janeiro. (2017). *Processo de autos n° 0504048-77.2017.4.02.5101; Autos n° 0503012-97.2017.4.02.5101.*

Ministério Público Federal & Procuraduria da Repúliba no Estado do Rio de Janeiro. (2016). *Processo de autos n° 0509503-57.2016.4.02.5101.* Source: http://politica.estadao.com.br/blogs/fausto-macedo/wp-content/uploads/sites/41/2017/11/75959255-1233-1-pp.pdf

Ministério Público Federal. (2014). *TERMO DE PRÉ-ACORDO DE COLABORAÇÃO PREMIADA.* Procuradoria-Geral Da República.

Minstério Público Federal. (2016). *PROCESSO No 0502834-85.2016.4.02.51011.* PROCURADORIA DA REPÚBLICA NO ESTADO DO RIO DE JANEIRO. Núcleo de Combate à Corrupção – Força Tarefa.

Morselli, C. (2008). *Inside Criminal Networks.* Montreal: Springer.

Mota Prado, M., Carson, L., & Correa, I. (2015). The Brazilian Clean Company Act: Using Institutional Multiplicity for Effective Punishment. *Osgoode Legal Studies Research Paper, 48.*

Paraguassu, L., & Soto, A. (May 10, 2016). Brazil's Temer calls for unity, confidence for Brazil recovery. *Reuters.* Source: https://www.reuters.com/article/us-brazil-politics/brazils-temer-calls-for-unity-confidence-for-brazil-recovery-idUSKC-N0Y206H

Pardo, I. (2004). *Between Morality and the Law: Corruption, Anthropology and Comparative Society* . Aldershot: Ashgate.

Pew Global. (2014). *Brazilian Discontent Ahead of World Cup.* Source: http://www.pewglobal.org/2014/06/03/brazilian-discontent-ahead-of-world-cup/

Pizzorno, A. (1992). La corruzione nel sistema político. Em D. Porta, *Lo Scambio Occult.* Bologna: Il Mulino.

Praça, S. (2011). Corrupção e reforma institucional no Brasil, 1988-2008. *Opiniao Publica. Vol. 17 Issue 1,* 137-162.

Radil, S. M., Flint, C., & Tita, G. E. (2010). Spatializing Social Networks: Using Social Network Analysis to investigate Geographies of Gang Rivarly, Territoriality and Violence in Los Angeles. *Annals of the Association of American Geographers, 100(2),* 307-326.

Rose-Ackerman, S. (1999). *Corruption and Government: Causes, Consequences and Reforms.* New York: Cambridge University Press.

Rufyikiri, G. (2016). Grand Corruption in Burundi: a collective action problem which poses major challenges for governance reforms. *Institute of Development Policy (IOB).*

Salcedo-Albarán, E., & Garay, L. J. (2012). *Narcotráfico, corrupción y Estados* . Bogotá: Debate.

Salcedo-Albarán, E., & Garay Salamanca, L. J. (2015). *Drug Trafficking, Corruption and States: How Illicit Netoworks Shaped Institutions in Colombia, Guatemala and México.* iUniverse.

Salcedo-Albarán, E., & Garay Salamanca, L. J. (2016). *Macro-criminalidad. Complejidad y resiliencia de las redes criminales.*Vortex Foundation and Small Wars

Journal. Bloomington:iUniverse.

Salcedo-Albarán, E., Goga, K., & Goredema, K. (2014). *Cape Town's underworld mapping a protection racket in the central business district.* Petroria: Institute for Security Studes.

Sapelli, G. (1998). *Cleptocracia. El "mecanismo" de la corrupción en política y eocnomía.* Buenos Aires: Ed. Losada S.A.

Serra, D., & Wantchekon, L. (2012). *New Advances in Experimental Research on Corruption.* Bingley: Emerald Group.

Sharafutdinova, G. (2010). What Explains Corruption Perceptions? The Dark Side of Political Competition in Russia's Regions. *Comparative Politics, 42*(2), 147-166.

Shiu Hing Lo, S. (2017). Comparative grand corruption and protection pacts among elites: the cases of Ao Man Long in Macao and Hui Si-Yan in Hong Kong. *Asian Journal of Political Science, 25*(2), 234-251.

Stanig, P. (2015). Regulation of Speech and Media Coverage of Corruption: An Empirical Analysis of the Mexican Press. *American Journal of Political Science, 59*(1), 175-193.

Stockemer, D., LaMontagne, B., & Scruggs, L. (2013). Bribes and ballots: The impact of corruption on voter turnout in democracies. *International Political Science Review / Revue internationale de science politique, 34*(1), 74 - 90.

Tverdova, Y. V. (2011). See No Evil: Heterogeneity in Public Perceptions of Corruption. *Canadian Journal of Political Science / Revue canadienne de science politique, 44*(1), 1-25.

V, d. B., & Segers, M. (2013). Transfer of Training: Adding Insight Through Social Network Analysis.

Educational Research Review(8), 34-47.

Villoria, M., Van Ryzin, G., & Lavena, C. (2013). Social consequences of government corruption: A study of institutional disaffection in Spain. *Public Administration Review*(73).

Watts, J. (June 21, 2013). Brazil erupts in protest: more than a million on the streets. *The Guardian.* Source: https://www.theguardian.com/world/2013/jun/21/brazil-police-crowds-rio-protest

Weitz-Shapiro, R., & Winters, M. S. (2013). Lacking information or condoning corruption: When will voters support corrupt politicians? *Comparative Politics 45 (4)*, 418-436.

Williams, B. (2005). *In the Beginning was the Deed.* Princeton : Princeton Univ. Press.

Williams, R. (June de 1999). The New Politics of Corruption. *Third World Quarterly,* 20(3), 487-489.

Winters, M. S., & Weitz-Shapiro, R. (2013). Lacking Information or Condoning Corruption: When Do Voters Support Corrupt Politicians? *Comparative Politics,* 45(4), 418-436.

Worell, J., Wasko, M., & Johnstn, A. (2013). Social Network Analysis in Accounting Information Systems Research. *International Journal of Accounting Information Systems*(14), 127-137.

World Bank. (1997). *Helping Countries Combat Corruption: The Role of The World Bank.* Washington: World Bank.

World Bank. (2017). *World Development Indicators GDP Brazil.* Source: https://goo.gl/jcSgqt

Annex. Sources

The analysis began with the first four police operations (court decisions) at the first instance of investigation - Lava Jato, Dolce Vita, Bidone and Casablanca-, each one focused on a criminal organization run by defendants Carlos Habib Chater, Alberto Youseff, Nelma Kodama and Henrique Srour. Sources extracted from: http://lavajato.mpf.mp.br/atuacao-na-1a-instancia/decisoes-da-justica.

- Operação Lava Jato. Pedido De Busca E Apreensão Criminal Nº 5001438¬85.2014.404.7000/PR.

- Operação Dolce Vita. Pedido De Busca E Apreensão Criminal Nº 5001461¬31.2014.404.7000/PR.

- Operação Bidone Pedido De Busca E Apreensão Criminal Nº 5001438¬85.2014.404.7000/PR.

- Operação Casa Blanca Pedido De Busca E Apreensão Criminal Nº 5001443¬10.2014.404.7000/PR

Then, 29 sentences at the first and second instances of investigation of "Lava Jato" Operation were extracted from http://lavajato.mpf.mp.br/atuacao-na-1a-instancia/denuncias-do-mpf and processed. Sentences were processed instead of complaints, since the information collected at the beginning of the investigation, as well as the information provided by the witnesses, was later confirmed or denied during the prosecution process; therefore, the final sentences provide more reliable information as key components of the "judicial truth".

First Stage Sources

- Ação Penal Nº 5025687-03.2014.404.7000/PR.
- Ação Penal Nº 502569225.2014.4.04.7000/PR.
- Ação Penal Nº 502621282.2014.4.04.7000/PR.
- Ação Penal Nº 502624305.2014.404.7000/PR.
- Ação Penal Nº 5035707-53.2014.404.7000/PR.
- Ação Penal Nº 5047229-77.2014.4.04.7000/PR.

Second Stage Sources

- Ação Penal Nº 508337605.2014.4.04.7000/PR
- Ação Penal Nº 508336051.2014.4.04.7000/PR
- Ação Penal Nº 508335189.2014.4.04.7000/PR
- Ação Penal Nº 508340118.2014.4.04.7000/PR
- Ação Penal Nº 508325829.2014.4.04.7000/PR
- Ação Penal Nº 502742237.2015.4.04.7000/PR
- Ação Penal Nº 508383859.2014.4.04.7000/PR
- Ação Penal Nº 500732698.2015.4.04.7000/PR
- Ação Penal Nº 501233104.2015.4.04.7000/PR
- Ação Penal Nº 502312147.2015.4.04.7000/PR
- Processo Nº 5023162-14.2015.4.04.7000
- Ação Penal Nº 5023135-31.2015.4.04.7000/PR
- Ação Penal Nº 503652823.2015.4.04.7000/PR
- Ação Penal Nº 503947550.2015.4.04.7000/PR
- Ação Penal Nº 504524184.2015.4.04.7000/PR
- Ação Penal Nº 506157851.2015.4.04.7000/PR

- Ação Penal Nº 5029737¬38.2015.4.04.7000/PR
- Ação Penal Nº 501340559.2016.4.04.7000/PR
- Ação Penal Nº 502217978.2016.4.04.7000/PR
- Ação Penal Nº 503042478.2016.4.04.7000/PR
- Ação Penal Nº 5051606¬23.2016.4.04.7000/PR
- Ação Penal Nº 5030883¬80.2016.4.04.7000/PR
- Ação Penal Nº 5022182¬33.2016.4.04.7000/PR

The analysis was then complemented with court decisions and annexes of judicial processes, extracted from https://jota.info/lavajota/ and http://lavajato.mpf.mp.br/atuacao--na-1a-instancia/.

- Autos N° 2009.70.00.019131-5 Ação Penal
- Pedido De Busca E Apreensão Criminal Nº 5073475 13.2014.4.04.7000/PR
- Autos De Ação Penal Nº 5025699-17.2014.404.7000
- Contrarrazões, João Luiz Correia Argôlo Dos Santos, Sidney Rocha Peixoto – Oab/Al 6217
- Pedido De Prisão Preventiva Nº 5011708-37.2015.4.04.7000/Pr
- Termo de Colaboração Nº 1 que Presta Julio Gerin De Almeida Camargo
- Extrato Detalhado – Caso 001-Mpf-001360-10
- Autos Nº: 5023162-14.2015.4.04.7000
- Pedido De Quebra De Sigilo De Dados E/Ou Telefônic Nº 5031505-33.2014.404.7000/Pr
- Ação Penal Nº 5013405-59.2016.4.04.7000/Pr
- Autos Nº 5025692-25.2014.404.7000
- Autos Nº 5083401-18.2014.404.7000
- Apelação Criminal Nº 5026212-82.2014.4.04.7000/Pr
- Ofício Nº 8243851 Ação Penal Nº 5025699-17.2014.404.7000/Pr

- Anexo 5 – Legend

- Processo Administrativo Nº 13896.721116/2015-85. Termo De Verificação Fiscal

- Autos Originários Nº 5073475-13.2014.404.7000 Ipl Nº 5071698-90.2014.404.7000 (Camargo Correa) IPL nº 5053836-09.2014.404.7000 (UTC)

- Ofício Nº 8244356 Ação Penal Nº 5025699-17.2014.404.7000/PR

- Autos Nº 5023121-47.2015.404.7000

- Devolução de carta precatória devidamente cumprida. 40120162095521, 8664-37.2016_31-8.pdf 15/08/2016 14:43:06

- Autos Nº 5083351-89.2014.4.04.7000

- Autos Nº 5053845-68.2014.404.7000 e 5044866-20.2014.404.7000 (IPL referente à ENGEVIX), 5049557-14.2013.404.7000 (IPL originário), 5073475-13.2014.404.7000 (Buscas e Apreensões) e conexos

- Distribuição por dependência aos autos Nº 5049557-14.2013.404.7000 (IPL originário), 004996-31.2015.404.7000 (IPL referente a Mario Goes), 5085114-28.2014.404.7000 (Busca eApreensão RIOMARINE) e conexos.

- Relatório De Análise De Polícia Judiciária Nº 124/2016

- Autos Nº 50001965720154047000

- Informação Nº 036/2015-Delefin/Drcor/Sr/Dpf/PR

- Processo Nº 5027422-37.2015.4.04.7000

- Processo-Crime De Autos Nº 5037800-18.2016.404.7000

- Termo De Depoimento De Marcos Pereira Berti

- Denúncia No Inquérito Nº 2245

- Ofício N.º 8284027 Ação Penal Nº 5026243-05.2014.404.7000/PR

- Questão De Ordem Na Ação Penal 871 Paraná

- Autos De Ação Penal Nº 5047229-77.2014.404.7000

- Pedido De Prisão Preventiva Nº 5012323-27.2015.4.04.7000/PR

- Termo De Audiência Ação Penal N°5037800-18.2016.404.7000

- Ofício Nº 700000522775 Ação Penal Nº 5012331-04.2015.4.04.7000/PR

- Contrarrazões Ao Recurso De Apelação Mateus Coutinho De Sá Oliveira E José Ricardo Nogueira Breghirolli

- Pedido de Prisão Preventiva Nº 5004872-14.2016.4.04.7000/PR

- Texto com Redação Final. Conselho De Ética E Decoro Parlamentar. Reunião Nº: 979/2014 Data: 13/8/2014

- Termo de Declarações Que Presta Meire Bonfim Da Silva Poza

- Auto de Qualificação Interrogatório De: Luiz Cláudio Machado Ribeiro

- Referência: Ação Penal Nº 5026663-10.2014.404.7000, Carlos Habib Chater Abdogado

- Pedido De Busca E Apreensão Criminal Nº 5004257-58.2015.4.04.7000/PR

- Ação Penal Nº 5061578-51.2015.4.04.7000/Pr. Ofício Nº 700001435567.

- Pedido De Busca E Apreensão Criminal Nº 5014497-09.2015.4.04.7000/Pr

- Pedido De Quebra De Sigilo De Dados E/Ou Telefônic Nº 5026387-13.2013.404.7000/Pr

- Pedido De Quebra De Sigilo De Dados E/Ou Telefônic Nº 5073645-82.2014.404.7000/Pr

- Autos Nº 5003682-16.2016.404.7000

- Exceção De Incompetência Criminal Nº 5022869-44.2015.4.04.7000/Pr

- Apelação Criminal Nº 5023162-14.2015.4.04.7000/Pr

- 21/06/2016 Segunda Turma Inquérito 3.997 Distrito Federal

- Registros 0088693 Nestor Cunat Cervero

- Solicitação De Assistência Jurídica Em Matéria Penal – Saj Nº 700000454378

- Ação Penal Nº 5083351-89.2014.4.04.7000/Pr Ofício Nº 700000424021

- Para distribuição por dependência aos autos nº 5046019-54.2015.4.04.7000 (Representação Criminal), nº 5047925-79.2015.404.7000 (Inquérito Policial) e nº 5049557-14.2013.404.7000 (Inquérito Bidone).

- IPL 0014808-07.2013.403.6120

- Ação Penal Nº 5045241-84.2015.4.04.7000

- Autos Nº 50001965720154047000

- Pedido De Busca E Apreensão Criminal Nº 5012298-77.2016.4.04.7000/Pr

- Serviço Publico Federal Mj – Polícia Federal – Sede Termo De Declarações De Paulo César Roxo Ramos

- Resposta À Acusação Ação Penal Nº 5013405-59.2016.4.04.7000

- Ação Penal 470 Minas Gerais

- Relatório De Polícia Judiciária Nº 010/16 Análise De Mídia Apreendida

- Referência: Ofício No 4001 -201s Dpf – Lpl 131 Stz014-4 Sr/Dpf/Pr

- Autos Nº 5012331-04.2015.404.7000

- Pedido De Busca E Apreensão Criminal Nº 5073475-13.2014.404.7000/Pr

- Os Pedidos De Prisão E Condução Coercitiva Folha-press

- Pedido De Busca E Apreensão Criminal Nº 5014455-57.2015.4.04.7000/Pr

- Translation Leonardo Meirelles E-Mail

- Comptes Bancaires Utilisés Dans La Dernière Couche Des Opérations De Blanchiment.n Ministère Public Fédéral.

- Ação Penal Nº 5049898-06.2014.404.7000/Pr

- Pedido De Busca E Apreensão Criminal Nº 5085114-28.2014.404.7000/Pr

- Autos Nº 5053744-31.2014.404.7000 (Ipl Referente À Mendes Júnior), 5073475- 13.2014.404.7000 (Buscas E Apreensões), 5049557-14.2013.404.7000 (Autos Originais) E Conexos.

- Pedido De Quebra De Sigilo De Dados E/Ou Telefônic Nº 5009225-34.2015.4.04.7000/Pr

- Documento Interno Do Sistema Petrobras – Dip

- Termo De Depoimento De Marcos Pereira Berti

- Pedido De Quebra De Sigilo De Dados E/Ou Telefônic Nº 5029786-79.2015.4.04.7000/Pr

- Habeas Corpus N.º 5029560-25.2015.404.0000

- Informação Nº 96/2014 Qualificação – Contatos Youssef – Utc/Constran Data: 15/10/2014

- Autos Nº: 5014455-57.2015.404.7000

- Autos N° 5039475-50.2015.4.04.7000

- Exceção De Litispendência Nº 5052022-59.2014.404.7000/Pr

- Termo De Transcrição Audiência Do Dia 19/02/2004

- Autos Nº 5036518-76.2015.4.04.7000/Pr

- Pedido De Busca E Apreensão Criminal Nº 5055178-21.2015.4.04.7000/Pr

- Anexo 05) Termo De Transcrição Dos Interrogatórios Dos Coacusados Na Ação Penal No 502569917.2014.404.7000

Sub-structures

Finally, the analysis of sub-structures was complemented with the following documents extracted from:

- Distribuçao por Dependência Aos Autos N° 0506973-80.2016.4.02.5101 – Quebra De Sigilos Bancário E Fiscal

- N° 108397/2017 – Gtlj-Pgr Inquérito N° 3995/Df

- Processo a ser Distribuido por Dependencia Aos Autos N° 0501018-34.2017.4.02.5101

- Distribuçao Por Dependência:

- Autos N° 053012-97-2017.4.02.5101 – homologacao de colaboracao premiada

- Autos N° 0503104-75.2017.4.02.5101 – prisao preventiva

- Autos N° 0502479-41.2017.4.02.5101 – quebra telemática

- Autos N° 0502500-17.2017.4.02.5101 – quebra de sigilos bancário/fiscal

- Autos N° 0503213-89.2017.4.02.5101 – quebra datos telefónicos

- Autos N° 0503229-43.2017.4.02.5101 – interceptacao

- Autos N° 0503211-22.2017.4.02.5101 – medida cautelar de sequestro

- Autos N° 0503212-07.2017.4.02.5101 – busca e apreensao

- Autos N° 0503371-47.2017.4.02.5101 – busca e apreensao complementar

- Autos N° 0503435-57.2017.4.02.5101 – inquerito policial (IPL 37/2017)

- Processo a ser distribuído por dependencia aos autos n°0503012-97.2017.4.02.5101

- Processo N° 0503104-75.2017.4.02.5101

- Processo N° 0502834-85.2016.4.02.5101

- Distribucao por dependencia: Processo N° 0210926-86.2015.4.02.5101

- Processo de autos N° 0504048-77.2017.4.02.5101

- Processo a ser distribuido por dependencia aos autos N° 0503012-97.2017.4.02.2101

- Processo de autos N° 0504048-77.2017.4.02.5101

- Processo a ser distribuido por dependencia aos autos N° 0503012-97.2017.02.5110

- Distribucao por dependencia aos autos N° 5006617-

- 29.2016.4.04.7000/PR Ref. Inquérito Policial N° 5006597-38.2016.4.04.7000

- Acao Penal N° 5046512-94.2016.4.04.7000/Pr

- Processo N° 12393-69.2017.4.01.3500

- Processo N° 12393-69.2017.4.01.3500

- Caso "De Volta Aos Trilhos" Ipl N° 0533/2013-4 Sr/Dpf/Go

- Ipl 0017513-21.2014.4.02.5101 Distribuzao Por Dependencia: Autos N°0057817-33.2012.4.02.5101 (Operacao Saqueador) E 0509503-57.2016.4.02.5101 (Operación Calicute)

- Processo N° 0017513.21.2014.4.02.5101

- (2014.51.01.017513-9).